SHIFT
HAPPENS

SHIFT HAPPENS

America's PremierExperts®
Reveal Their Biggest Secrets
to Help You Thrive in the New Economy

featuring

America's
PremierExperts®

Published by CelebrityPress™, Orlando, FL
A division of The Celebrity Branding® Agency

Celebrity Branding® is a registered trademark
Printed in the United States of America.

ISBN: 9780615322483
LCCN: 2009938197

This publication is designed to provide accurate and authoritative information with regard to the subject matter covered. It is sold with the understanding that the publisher is not engaged in rendering legal, accounting, or other professional advice. If legal advice or other expert assistance is required, the services of a competent professional should be sought.

Most CelebrityPress™ titles are available at special quantity discounts for bulk purchases for sales promotions, premiums, fundraising, and educational use. Special versions or book excerpts can also be created to fit specific needs.

For more information, please write:

CelebrityPress™,
520 N. Orlando Ave, #44,
Winter Park, FL 32789

or call 1.800.980.1626

Visit us online at www.**CelebrityBrandingAgency**.com

CONTENTS

SHIFT HAPPENS

America's PremierExperts®
Reveal Their Biggest Secrets
to Help You Thrive in the New Economy

Editors: J.W. Dicks, Esq. and Nick Nanton, Esq.

INTRODUCTION

Shift *Does* Happen...and Why You Should Care

If you live in a city and spend any commuting time on the highway, you've seen those annoying drivers – the ones that are doing everything but paying attention to the road. It might be the woman applying eyeliner or blush or the guy forwarding to the next track on his iPod or someone who forgot to put the Splenda in her latte at Starbucks. And what's with those guys who forgot to shave at home?

Our BlackBerrys and iPhones distract us from the big picture: we're in a speeding car that can turn into a deadly weapon on a dime. The minute we fail to pay attention, tragedy can strike. We may have avoided it today, but tomorrow could be another story. We're always pushing our luck.

It's the same with our constantly shifting economy. If we keep focusing on silly distractions, continue to do business the way we've been doing it, and fail to see the big picture or anticipate the curves in the road ahead, we're bound to crash, or at the very least, stall.

Let's face facts. These days, we're trying to keep pace with a coming-at-the-speed-of-light era characterized by a batch of realities we didn't have to think about just a few years ago: globalization and universal competition, lightning-quick exchange of information, and business models that become more and more fascinating yet also complex at the same time. All of these technological advances have led to a whole new way of thinking about business and consumers whose attention span, like that of those frenzied drivers, sometimes rivals that of a buzzing insect.

Remember those great TV theme songs you grew up with? They're mostly a thing of the past now because every second counts. If a show doesn't hook you in within a minute, the corporations that run the networks know you'll change the channel to any one of a hundred different satellite stations. Or you'll go online or pop in a DVD. They think you're fickle, but the truth is, as a consumer you have all the power – because you have *options*.

So these days, when you're the one in business, you have to recognize consumer trends and anticipate change – or else. It's simple natural selection, actually. Charles Darwin lived long before the automobile was invented, but we can take a lesson from him. He said, "It's not the strongest nor most intelligent of the species that survive; it is the one most adaptable to change."

Are you miffed that the government is tampering with this law, using your tax dollars to bail out or declare bankruptcy for our American car companies to save them from total collapse and the loss of hundreds of thousands of jobs? Aren't these companies run by the best and brightest corporate minds? We thought so, but apparently GM and Chrysler were just thinking bigger and better. They didn't anticipate the fluctuating gas prices of the past few years and the American consumer's desire to drive more energy- and cost-efficient vehicles.

Our banks pretty much did the same thing, giving into the greedy, high-on-the-hog mentality that inspired them to lend money to barely qualified homebuyers who had no down payment to lose if they defaulted. When the economy faltered, the banks were left holding the bag. Forsaking any sort of regulation or restrictions, they created a market of overinflated, bloated values based on products and services that ultimately weren't good. The bubble was bound to burst. They didn't see it coming, but they should have.

The Rise and Fall of the Newspaper Empire

Let's take a look at the perfect example of the shrinking, some would say dying, newspaper industry. The morning paper, the tangible item the paperboy throws at your door with newsprint that runs on your hands, has been a staple of American life since the country started. It's still there for those who want it, but again, the so-called brilliant minds running these massive organizations are in severe economic trouble because they've been slow to adapt to the changing realities of the tech age.

Ironically, it's the news industry that reports the bad news every day. First *The New York Times* dumps one hundred jobs. Then the crippled Tribune Company is downsizing and laying off hundreds of people. There are constant reports of dipping conventional advertising dollars. AdAge recently reported that in December 2008, U.S. media employment fell to a fifteen-year low (886,900), slammed by the slumping newspaper industry. But employment in advertising/marketing services – agencies and other firms that provide marketing and communications services to marketers – broke an upward record in November (769,000).

Could it really be true? Can it be that nobody's reading newspapers anymore? Yes and no. No to the tangible foldovers you buy at the newsstand, but yes to their online editions. It's just that the news industry is shifting into the online world. A report in *Editor & Publisher* claims that the online audience is indeed "soaring."

Let's check the stats. Here are the growth rate and numbers of unique readers for newspaper Web sites in early 2008:

- NYTimes.com: 20,461,000 – 45.1%

- USAToday.com: 12,314,000 – 19.4%

- WashingtonPost.com: 9,902,000 – 14.6%

- Wall Street Journal Online: 6,962,000 – 81.4%

- LATimes.com: 5,715,000 – 4.7%

Not only are these huge audiences, but the growth rates continue to be spectacular – and bigger by far now, over a year later. If we look down the list, number 16, the *Seattle Post-Intelligencer*, has a unique Web audience of 2.2 million. Yet the paper's print circulation, when it was considered healthy in the last century, was somewhere in the low two hundred thousands. This low print number has led to decreased ad revenue, major financial losses, staff layoffs, and lower quality content. As the paper's content has degraded, the perception of it in the community is one of declining influence and quality.

We are seeing a major trend where many American cities will be left with one daily newspaper and some, perhaps, with none within a couple of years. Because the publishing industry failed to see the changes coming and figure out a way to adjust and thrive in today's complex world, a lot of legendary papers are turning into yesterday's news.

On February 27, 2009, the 149-year-old *Rocky Mountain News* published its last edition after the owner-company, E.W. Scripps, could not find a buyer and decided to leave Colorado for good. Think of it. The *Rocky Mountain News* survived the Civil War, the Spanish-American War, the First World War, the Great Depression, the Second World War, the Korean War, the Cold War, the Vietnam War, Watergate, etc., having been witness to many of the seminal events of the past two centuries. Yet it could not survive in the new era of information exchange.

Conventional wisdom says that newspapers are caught in a business model that doesn't support the changes to digital media, and despite huge efforts, the newspaper industry is in decline. Maybe there's no longer a place for traditional newspapers. Or so they say.

But the truth is, they failed to invest in themselves so that they could compete in the digital age. Most digital operations are seriously understaffed and under-resourced. They failed to employ those basic traffic-building strategies that independents are using with great success. Want innovation? Turn to eBay, Craigslist, Google, Yahoo, and Monster.com. Oh yes, and all those wildly successful ad networks that have siphoned away customers.

Thousands of tiny but mighty Web operations have sprung up to compete with traditional newspapers, and what did the stodgy papers do? They thought they knew better, so they stayed stuck and sinking with their old business models. Reporters and editors who should be incorporating the digital world into their basic job descriptions are instead looking at technology as something to add on to their conventional reporting – when they can find the time.

Meanwhile, who is succeeding in the world of information exchange?

You guessed it. Facebook, Twitter, Myspace, Linked In…for starters. Social networks have signed up hundreds of millions of users, and people are turning to bloggers for truth, opinions, and advice. Some are making so much money that they're hiring their own editors and reporters and winning awards.

You instinctively know what it takes to survive and thrive in the New Economy. If you're a smart businessperson, it's pure instinct. It's all about understanding globalization, predicting and responding smartly to the dizzying changes (yes, you can keep pace and outrun the competition with a little ingenuity), and of course, knowledge. There's no greater a strategic factor in business than intellectual capital.

Don't be like those newspapers! Being open to learning on a continuous basis is one of the key elements of success. These days, knowledge is the foremost component of customer value. Those who seek, absorb, and manage knowledge the most effectively are the ones who will blast away their competition. And don't forget the Internet, which, for those savvy enough to figure it out, has changed the fundamental nature of doing business.

As innovative ways of creating and delivering your products and services become available, take advantage of the technology to get the word out to the world. Our ability to access incredible amounts of information within seconds and to communicate across the globe for next to nothing has changed the way human beings and companies interact. Distance is a shrinking barrier, and the days of building a customer base near your geographic location are over. A recent report says that the world trade economy is growing at more than five times the rate of world gross domestic product.

While business owners who plug into the changing realities of the modern world can thrive, we all must realize that we only exist because of the consumer. The customer has all the power these days. Globalization has led more companies to pursue the same customers. At the same time, those consumers have been more informed and have become more sophisticated because they have so many options. They've also benefitted because of information technology, which allows them to compare products with a few simple mouse clicks. They're making more informed choices. Again, it's about *options* – and they're holding out for the best one.

Because of the glut of products out there, sometimes it's a monumental challenge for you as a business owner to differentiate yourself from your competitors. But it's not impossible – as long as you're open-minded and ready to embrace your bright and lucrative future.

You can do it – and we have compiled the brightest minds across many diverse industries to show you how. We asked them all to share how they were surviving and thriving in their own businesses in the current economy, so you could learn not only from theory but also from practical application.

We hope you enjoy reading the book as much as we enjoyed the exciting process of putting it together. The valuable information found in this anthology will not teach you how to *endure* the current economic shift, it shows you how to *prosper* within it.

Because shift happens, we are dedicated to helping you revel in it,

JW Dicks, Esq. & Nick Nanton, Esq.

FIRST, DECIDE THAT SUCCESS IS THE ONLY OPTION. THEN, DO NOT WAIVER.

by Jennifer Myers

Without a doubt, it is a challenge to thrive in today's business environment. But sometimes what at first seems like the worst of times can end up being the best of times for the determined business owner. If you're like me and decide to go into business for yourself, you first have to *decide* that you want to succeed. You have to *decide* that there are no other options – you *have* to make your business work.

I'm a real estate agent in DC, Maryland, and Virginia. The residential real estate market has been hit especially hard, but I'm still consistently one of the highest-ranking agents in my area. But that doesn't mean things haven't been difficult.

Change Is Constant, DO Something About It!

When I first started in real estate, the market was booming and no one had to be convinced that buying a home was something they should do. But, then the market changed and people became fearful. Buyers were suddenly gone and sellers couldn't sell their homes.

When the going got tough, I had to remind myself that I had to consciously choose every day to be successful. What goes up must come down. The hay days were over, as we all knew they would be eventually. So what activities could I do every day to run a successful business now that things had change so drastically and so quickly?

I decided to ask myself several questions to help me decide how I was going to cope with this changed environment: What was I truly passionate about? Why had I chosen years before to quit my nice, steady paycheck of a job and start a real estate business in the first place? What did I want to accomplish with my work? What could I give back to people? And the most important question of all: What knowledge or experience did I possess that set me apart from my competition? What would make people seek me out and pay me for that expertise?

As Dan Kennedy, the "Millionaire-Maker," always says, customers and clients are always asking, "What's in it for me?" You have to answer that question unequivocally for them. Your job as a successful entrepreneur, if you so choose to accept it, is to convince them that what you have to offer is better than choosing someone/something else or doing nothing at all. Dan Kennedy taught me that, too.

Find Your Passion and Riches Will Follow

Most importantly, you first need your business to revolve around one of your passions in life. What makes you want to go to work, what makes you excited, and what just naturally seems the right fit for you? I found my passion working in real estate in my early twenties. I intuitively understood that real estate, if done responsibly, was the best financial tool for building wealth. So, I decided to jump into the game and buy my first home at twenty-two.

I later found out that I could have saved fifty thousand dollars through a housing assistance program for first-time buyers. No one had told me about this free money the government was giving away to first-time homebuyers. I was shocked that the experts I hired to help me didn't even know about these programs that I would have benefited so greatly from. But, it was too late for me because I had already bought my first home.

Deciding I didn't want that to happen to other first-time buyers, I switched careers and made it my mission as a real estate agent to keep my clients informed and show them the way to an affordable home. I am now the author of a forthcoming book due out in late 2009 that will explain to first-time homebuyers about all the free money available to them to purchase their first home. It is called **"ON THE HOUSE: How To Find Free Government Money To Make Your First Home Affordable".**

I went into real estate genuinely wanting to help people find homes they would love but could also afford. Because of this, my clients realize that I don't just see them as dollar signs but always act in their best interests, not my own. I didn't go into real estate because I thought I could get rich quick. If you feel this way about what you do, customers or clients will sense your sincere passion and want to work with you. Ask yourself if you would be in the same field if you weren't getting paid. Then you know you've found your passion! And when you are doing something you love every day, you'll have more success and money than you could ever dream possible. That I know for sure.

Get Out of Your Own Way!

There are probably 1,001 reasons why you can't be successful, can't win, can't get the clients or customers you want, can't afford to invest in the business, can't, can't, can't! Put the excuses aside and decide to get out of your own way. Focus instead on the activities you *can* do day-in and day-out that are going to get you the results and success you desire. Focusing on all the reasons you can't be successful will get you nowhere quick.

When I first started in real estate, my biggest obstacle was my age. I was only twenty-three years old and looked even younger! Older clients would always comment how young I looked, ask me my age, and act hesitant to work with me. I let this hold me back at first, and it gave me an excuse to fail: I was too young to succeed.

Then I started to realize that the clients I enjoyed working with and who enjoyed working with me were young like me. They related to me and trusted that I had their best interests at heart because I was just like them. I could offer them something that other agents couldn't – I was their confidant and friend and truly understood their needs and concerns about buying their first home. I enjoyed working with them, and they could sense my enthusiasm and genuine interest in them. We had fun during what could have been a very stressful experience, and so they told all their friends about their great experience and I kept multiplying my client base.

Once I *decided* to get out of my own way and *chose* not to listen to that head noise we all have about why this could never possibly work out, I suddenly had more clients then I knew what to do with, and I had to expand my team of people just to keep up with the volume of sales I was handling – all at a time when we were in the midst of the worst economy since the Great Depression and a real estate market taking a nosedive.

The Riches Are in the Niches

So, you've chosen to follow your passion and decided to get out of your own way, but something feels like it's still missing. It's not all clicking yet.

You feel like you can't figure out the details of how to make this all work and be systematized. There are too many options to choose from. What path do you take? The answer: you start by focusing on *one* target market.

In my own experience, something was still definitely missing. I was all over the place trying to please any client that came my direction. I was overworked and unhappy with the direction my business was heading. I couldn't answer that question of why people should choose to work with me above all their other options.

I spent at least a year asking myself this question every day. But what I didn't realize at first was that my business was exploding doing exactly that – giving away expert knowledge to young, first-time homebuyers about all the government programs, free money, tax incentives, and many other programs available only to them. They were coming to me because they knew I would find a program that fit their specific circumstances and get them the home they wanted more affordably than they could figure out on their own.

This was how I found a niche that others weren't serving and didn't have as much interest in working with, especially in the heady days of the real estate boom. Many agents at that time focused on luxury homes and subprime loans to get their clients the biggest houses (and them the biggest commissions). By choosing to focus only on this niche market of first-time buyers, whom I also enjoyed working with, I was able to provide even better service since I could keep up-to-date on assistance programs specific for them. I could really focus on their needs and get to know the ins and outs of this client base.

What was even better was that I was able to start saying no to clients who didn't fit my target market. I didn't enjoy working with them as much anyway because I felt I wasn't providing them with real value or that I was the best agent for what they needed. Because I had the confidence in my expertise within my niche market, I was able to be more selective with my clients and work only with those that fit what I did best – first-time homebuyers. At first, saying no to clients that didn't fit my target market was scary. I was turning down thousands of dollars. But strangely enough, I began to have more clients than ever.

Come from a Place of Constant Gratitude

When you face a time like this when the economy has shifted and the old rules no longer apply, you need to be thankful for the lessons that "bad times" teach.

If it weren't for the downturn in real estate and the economy as a whole, I would never have gotten where I am today. Only after the downturn and feeling frustrated by the new rules of real estate did I realize I most enjoyed working with first-time buyers. I now enjoy my business more than ever, and it is more profitable than ever before. In between helping first-time homebuyers, I also consult with investors on how to make huge profits flipping properties (yes, even in this "down" market). I do what I teach as well, buying several properties at foreclosure auctions per year and making no less than 25% ROI in ninety days on each flip.

None of these accomplishments would have been possible if I didn't first decide there was no Plan B to fall back on. Failing was not an option for me, so I chose to do things that would lead to a successful business every single day. This meant sometimes making very calculated decisions based on what I was most passionate about, which lead me to my perfect niche market and I've been thankful for the lesson the recent downturn have taught me ever since.

To find out more information or how to work with me, visit www.JenniferMyers.com.

ABOUT JENNIFER MYERS:

Jennifer Myers is undeniably an advocate and recognized expert for first-time homebuyers. Her new book, ***ON THE HOUSE Finding free government money to make your first home affordable***, chronicles a step-by-step formula that first-time buyers can use to receive grant money and other resources to help make their first home purchase more affordable.

Jennifer first became passionate about real estate in 2002 after buying her first home and later realizing she could have saved $50,000 through a housing assistance program. Ever since then, her mission has been to help others avoid that same mistake. She is the real estate agent that goes the extra step to inform her clients on how to find this money. A first-time buyer has only one time to take advantage of these opportunities and Jennifer leads them through this process.

Jennifer has worked with hundreds of clients. In fact, she was the top producer in her area during her first year as an agent. Her energetic determination and thirst for knowledge of the real estate market enables her to keep abreast of the latest housing information and keeps her on the front lines of the industry.

She also knows that owning your first home can be the largest financial investment you will make. She encourages responsible homeownership and works with her clients so that they find a home that meets both their needs and their pocketbooks. That first home is a stepping stone to your next home, so she truly believes you want to make it right the first time.

As a young homeowner herself, Jennifer knows first-hand the benefits of owning your own place. She wants to share that excitement and pride with others and relates to the concerns that young, first-time buyers may have. She believes that owning a home is not only a financial investment but a personal investment that will bring the owner many happy returns.

Jennifer Myers lives and works in the Washington, D.C., metropolitan area.

You can learn more about Jennifer, how to work with her, her books, courses, programs and services at JenniferMyers.com.

www.JenniferMyers.com

THAT PERSONAL TOUCH: PRESERVE YOUR CUSTOMER BASE

by Dr. Vesna Sutter, DDS

I t was a Friday night at 8:30 – not usually when you want to think about work.

But the phone rang and I answered. On the other end was a very upset mom. Her son had fallen on the playground and knocked out a tooth. Her regular dentist hadn't even answered his phone. Could I help?

My answer? "Of course."

That was the second time I'd suddenly found myself with a new family of patients – and a dentist who hadn't answered his phone had lost one.

I've been a dentist for over twenty years, and I've seen lots of economic shifts, although the current downturn is obviously one of the biggest. But I know everything goes in a cycle. The stock market goes down; it'll go back up. House prices go down; they'll go back up. You and I can't control that.

People, however, always remain a constant. And we *can* work on making those relationships as strong as possible.

My philosophy is that if you concentrate on creating new patient relationships as well as maintaining the ones you already have, you should withstand all economic stresses coming your way. People will stay loyal to you as long as possible – if you treat them with respect and care.

Back to that Friday night phone call. I didn't help out that mom just to get a new patient, and I honestly didn't treat her any differently than I would any other patient. In other words, I wasn't rubbing my hands together gleefully with an evil cackle as I imagined snatching this family away and into *my* patient database.

No, it's just the level of commitment I've genuinely felt towards my patients since I graduated from dental school. But that mom obviously thought I *did* go out of my way, and maybe she'll end up telling everyone she knows about how I helped her when her regular dentist made himself completely unavailable.

That's certainly not going to hurt my practice; word-of-mouth is the most powerful kind of marketing. How could it not be? It involves people getting referrals from other people they already know and trust. But, again, *that's not why I did it.*

Keeping Track

I believe any business that shows a genuine commitment to customer service – as well as a sincere caring for customers' needs – is going to do better than one that doesn't. And that's something that sustains a business through rough patches. Building customer loyalty and striving to meet their needs is the foundation of any successful enterprise. If you can't convert a new customer into an ongoing one, your business will quickly shrivel up and die.

Here's another example of making 'that personal touch' work for you. My husband is in the restaurant business, and he makes it a point to get to know the restaurant "regulars." That way he can greet them personally, and they feel at home. He knows who they are, what they do, and so on. And again, it's just how he approaches his business: he cares about the people who come and patronize his restaurant.

What sometimes happens is that we go out to another restaurant and we see one of those regulars. Oops, they're eating at someplace other than my husband's! But my husband is cool about it and he says hello to them by name – and they're reminded of him, his friendly attitude, and his restaurant. And they'll usually make it a point to come back to eat at his place after one of those encounters.

There are other ways to embed 'that personal touch' into the day-to-day operation of your business. In my practice, after patients leave, we often write down a few notes about what's happening in their lives as "memory joggers" for the next time we see them. Is there a wedding coming up in their family? A birth? A big anniversary or birthday? That way we don't lose track of their lives, and the next time they come to see us they know that we genuinely care about them.

We also do little things like sending out thank-you cards when they send referrals our way. They've done us a big favor, and it's nice to acknowledge that personally.

Now, I wasn't taught any of this in dental school. They were too busy concentrating on things like teeth and gums and teaching me how to be a "carpenter of the mouth." You know, the stuff a dentist needs to know? But what they don't teach you in dental school, or in almost any other school, for that matter, are business fundamentals like how to communicate with your customers, patients, or clients. Learning this as well as how to motivate your office team so everyone's on the same page is essential to run a successful practice.

That's why from the beginning I made it a point to broaden my perspective beyond looking into people's mouths. I go to ten to fifteen seminars a year to educate myself about different aspects of my practice: motivational workshops and business management, customer communication, and marketing sessions - in addition, of course, to seminars on dentistry itself. Making sure to go beyond your core occupation to understand the latest thinking in marketing, motivation, and management, I believe, is essential – because I'm not just a dentist, I'm also a business owner. And it's up to me to obtain the additional skills it takes to fulfill that role as well as I can.

Expanding my education into the management and communication areas hasn't just helped with my practice, by the way. It's also helped me be a better wife and mother. Boosting your skills in those areas helps your interactions with your family and helps you to manage your personal life better as well. Improving my personal life and becoming more comfortable with myself has brought me more happiness – and the happier you are in all areas of life, the happier you are in your business and how you relate to your clients (again, in my case, my patients). If you come in growling like a 'stress monster', that's not going to foster good vibrations. That's not to say I don't have a bad day now and then, but I certainly get through them a lot easier.

Adding Value

Another way I believe you help foster customer loyalty is to bring added value to them any way you can. In my case, I began treating my patients for sleep apnea (a sleep disorder caused by pauses in breathing). This isn't a big moneymaker for me, but it's something I enjoy doing because it makes a huge difference in people's lives.

For instance, my assistant's husband had the problem. He always snored, he didn't have very restful sleep, and as a result he was very lethargic during the day. I helped treat him, and it totally changed his life. He said to me, "I feel great, and I just can't believe how long the days are" because now he has the energy to give it his all.

Treating sleep apnea was a natural addition to my services; when I initially examine a new patient, it's easy to screen for airway passage problems at the same time. It didn't detract from my core business, and it provided an amazing level of satisfaction both on my end and my patients' when I was able to identify the disorder and successfully treat it.

I love being able to help people in a substantial way. To see the positive impact you can have on someone's life makes your work more enjoyable and fosters a great atmosphere at your workplace. Yes, root canals are necessary, and yes, people need them; but what's more exciting is changing someone's smile and helping boost their confidence and their attitude on a long-term basis.

In today's economy, that smile – and that confidence – is important. People are losing jobs they've had with companies for thirty and forty years. They need to look and feel as good about themselves as they can when they go out to find a new position in a difficult climate. If you feel good about yourself, you can bet other people will feel good about you, too, because when times are tough you need every edge you can get.

Naturally, 'that personal touch' can't cure all economic ills. At the moment, I have to tell my team at my practice that, yes, we've got more openings than normal, and yes, our revenues might go down a bit, but if we keep focusing on the basics and doing what we do best, we'll ride the wave and ultimately be fine.

In the meantime, we should all remember that what we give, we eventually get back. Over the years, I've come to regard many of my patients as my friends. One woman whom I helped with both her sleep apnea and her smile through cosmetic dentistry took to improving the quality of her diet and started grinding her own wheat. Now she brings me in her own homemade flour, which I take home and use to bake the most delicious bread I've ever tasted.

When your patients bring *you* gifts, you know you're doing something right!

ABOUT DR. VESNA SUTTER, DDS:

Dr. Vesna S. Sutter has been creating beautiful and healthy smiles for her patients for the past twenty years. She is a 1986 graduate of Loyola Dental School and completed her undergraduate studies at University of Illinois at Urbana-Champaign.

Since completing her formal education, Dr. Sutter has taken over 500 hours of continuing education in Orthodontics, TMJ Disorders, Cosmetic Dentistry, Implants, Sedation, and Sleep Disorder Dentistry.

She is an active member of several professional organizations:

Dental Organization for Conscious Sedation (DOCS)

American Academy of Cosmetic Dentistry

American Dental Association

Chicago Dental Society

Illinois State Dental Society

American Association of Functional Orthodontics

International Association for Orthodontics

Academy of Dental Sleep Medicine

American Academy of Sleep Medicine

North American Neuromuscular Study Club

Dr. Sutter lives in South Barrington with her husband and two children. In her spare time she enjoys cooking, decorating and outdoor activities.

Dr. Sutter believes in providing the highest quality of oral health care and whole body wellness in a relaxed and comfortable environment. She is devoted to helping her patients achieve the smile and health they have been striving for.

For more information, please visit:

www.SunriseDentalCare.com

PROSPER FROM THE SHIFT: THE SAFEST PLACE TO INVEST

by Ron Caruthers
with Ed Sanderson

I f we've learned anything from the recent stock market woes, it's that there is only one 'surefire' place to invest that will succeed 100% of the time, and that's yourself. Benjamin Franklin said it best: "If a man empties his purse into his head, no man can take it away from him. An investment in knowledge always pays the best interest."

Right now, an old economy is crumbling around us. People who had huge success in the real estate market for a few years and own a number of rental properties are getting crushed by the debts on those properties. Blue chip stocks that were dependable for years have plummeted in value recently and in some cases may never return to their original price levels.

Even the auto industry that America built has completely fallen apart; the companies are being sold to foreign companies or are requiring massive government bailouts to remain viable.

So, how do you avoid being another casualty in business any time a major shift happens? By investing in yourself, in your own skills, talents, and field to remain competent and competitive.

In this life, *you* are the only thing that you can truly count on, so *you* are the only thing worth truly investing in. So, let's explore some of the best places to start.

1. Invest in your attitude.

One thing that the Multi-Level Marketing (MLM) industry has right is that you need a great attitude to get anything done. One of their core principles of business is to spend thirty minutes a day reading something educational and inspirational. For years I enjoyed associating with one of those groups, not because I ever expected to get rich from it but simply because I enjoyed the tapes and books that they exposed me to.

I try very hard to stick to two habits in this area. First, I start every morning with the "Leaders & Success" page of *Investors Business Daily*. This newspaper devotes a whole page each day to profiling a different business, political leader, or sports leader and what made them successful. They also have a daily column that focuses on one of the ten traits of successful people they've identified. It only takes a few minutes to read, but it gets me in an excellent mood for the day ahead. I highly recommend it, and you can get a two-week free trial by going to www.Investors.com.

I also try to read a book a week, especially biographies of successful individuals like Donald Trump or Richard Branson. I've gone through some tough times recently with a couple of personal "shifts" of my own, and reading about how other people have overcome challenges is always encouraging. I was almost half a million dollars in debt because of a divorce. However, reading about Donald Trump being nine *billion* dollars in debt at one point in his life helped to give me perspective on it and, at the very least, feel more equipped to handle my own situation. Everything is relative, right? Reading that story of his as detailed in his books really helped give me the right attitude about my own problems.

2. Invest in your marketing knowledge.

When hard times hit, one of the first things that most business owners tend to do is circle the wagons. They begin to look for ways to cut expenses and lower costs, rather than acting boldly and decisively and going after their competitors to drive them out of business.

So, you should always be spending time and money learning new and better ways to promote your business and attract new clients. One of the best things I ever heard was marketing expert Jeff Paul asking a room full of financial planners what business they were in. They all responded with some version of saying they were in the financial planning business. Jeff then told them they all were wrong. To be successful, they had to be in the *marketing business*. Until they made the shift mentally from being in the business of financial planning to being in the business of *marketing* financial planning services, they would always have a mediocre practice.

So, how many new ways did you learn last year or last month to promote your business or practice to your audience? You need to learn how to use all avenues to get as many potential clients as possible to learn about you. When marketing guru Dan Kennedy was asked about one specific thing anyone could do to get a hundred new clients, his answer was "I don't know any *one* thing to do to get one hundred new clients, but I do know one hundred different ways that will each get me one new client, *and I use them all."*

So, here are just a few of the areas you want to pay attention to:

- how to get positive PR for your business

- how to use the Internet profitably

- how to use the local Chamber of Commerce

- how to use direct mail

- how to get your existing clients to refer more often to you

- how to have your staff constantly market for you

Again, learning about each of these areas is an investment, because each can be managed so that they are a *true* investment, giving a true return. For example, once you've learned how to use direct mail profitably, you can comfortably mail as often as you want because you know that each dollar spent will always return two, three, four, or even ten dollars to you. Try getting that type of return in the stock market all the time!

And, of course, there are people who know a ton about each of these subjects, so it comes back to investing in yourself through them: buy their experience so you can shortcut your own learning curve.

We run www.CollegePlanningSpecialists.com, a Web site that helps parents prepare their students for college while teaching them how to get thousands of free dollars for the school of their choice. Recently, we followed someone else's advice on how to promote this business. A one-hour phone call with a small amount of promotion yielded us $118,000 in additional sales....all because we took the time and money to invest a relatively modest sum with someone who had done this dozens of times before. That person gave me the keys and shortcuts to turbo-charge our success.

In many ways, it's why people hire us to get their own college planning businesses off the ground. We're not cheap. In fact, we charge a small fortune to help them, but we're able to save them years of frustration and stumbling making their own mistakes because we have sixteen years of experience. I'm generally able to make a business profitable within six months when it would normally take two to three years. So, even though we're expensive, we're worth it to save two years of fumbling about.

3. Invest in true experts in financial and legal matters.

No one person can know everything, so it's worth your investment to have professionals help you in areas in which you're not an expert.

For instance, even though I have a tax and accounting background, my CPA is an invaluable asset to me. Because I specialize in the world of college planning, I no longer keep as current on the tax laws as I'd like to. Therefore, I rely on her to keep me up to date on ways I can legally use my business to save me as much money as possible on what I owe the government. The couple of thousands of dollars that I spend with her each year save me tens of thousands at tax time...again, a return you can't make every year in the real estate or equity markets.

I also see this all the time in my own practice. Families come to me for my specialized knowledge about the college planning process. I help them figure out how to help their kids focus so they come out in the least amount of time possible with a degree and a job in the real world, *and* I show them how to get thousands of free dollars along the way. They spend money with me, but I save much more money for them.

I could name almost any of the 2,600 families that I've personally worked with, but one experience in particular comes to mind. A single mom who owns a homeopathy business came to me right about the time her second son was starting his college applications. Her first son was a junior at a private university and wasn't getting a dime of financial aid, even though her tax preparer had helped her with his financial aid paperwork.

However, because I'm the expert in this field, I quickly realized that he'd made a number of mistakes, which had cost them money. I jumped into action to fix the issues, and we were able to secure $22,490 a year free at the University of California school that her second son decided to attend. Not only that, I helped them get another $15,700 free for her older son's final year!

So, even though she invested almost five thousand dollars with me, she received back $105,660 over four years, a whopping 2,013% return on investment. And she got the satisfaction of telling her ex-husband that she didn't need a dime of his money to help put the boys through school. Her investment in my expertise really paid off.

4. Invest in your staff.

In contrast to so many businesses that are letting employees go left and right, we're now hiring some of the people the recession has left unemployed, and you would be wise to consider doing the same. This is the ideal climate in which to focus on building up areas that your company is weak in because you can find some "first-round draft picks" in the marketplace that weren't available before. We've recently added a full-time former admissions officer to help students better prepare to get in to college, and we've also added a full-time Web master, since the Internet is going to be such a huge part of our future business. Also, I've transferred one of my key employee's responsibilities to someone else so she could be my full-time personal assistant, allowing me to focus more of my time on what I do best.

Good staff will *always* make you more money than they cost you. Most small business owners stay that way because they focus on controlling costs and try to do everything themselves. Well, I hate to break it to you, but you'll never hit the big times if you're bogged down doing $15-an-hour work. You need to learn to think and act like a CEO, so you're going to need good staff to help maximize your time and value to your company.

Motivational broadcaster Earl Nightingale said that if you have no other success guide to go by, simply look at what everyone else around you is doing…and do the exact opposite. So, particularly during times of crisis or shift, make sure that you boldly and decisively move forward to take new ground while your competitors cower in fear. One of the best ways that you can do that is by constantly investing in yourself: your attitude, your marketing prowess, other professionals, and your staff.

Ken Roberts, the commodity trading guru, once said that if you took everything away from him and gave him only a lawn mower, within a year he would be making a six-figure income, because success ultimately is all about how you think and act, not your specific circumstances.

The greatest security in life is being so competent in all areas of your business that if you were dropped from an airplane anywhere in the country, within ninety days you would have rebuilt your business and made it successful. You only get that by investing in yourself.

ABOUT RON CARUTHERS:

Ron Caruthers is the nation's leading expert on getting into and paying for colleges-as well as helping students choose their careers and command top money in their fields. He is also well-known for helping families that didn't save enough for college get on track for their retirement.

He was born and raised in Santa Monica, California – right above 'Baywatch' beach. In fact, he was a Los Angeles County (Baywatch) lifeguard for two summers.

Ron graduated from Sunny Hills High School in Fullerton, CA in 1985. He graduated with top honors as the sole valedictorian of his class, being ranked number 1 out of 419 students. However, due to poor career planning and lack of finances, he did not immediately go on to college. In fact, 7 years later, this misfortune led to him researching the financial aid system, as well as taking a hard look into just how poorly most students were prepared for college and a career.

In 1995, Ron Caruthers launched his college planning company in Vista, CA. Since then, he has worked with over 2600 families helping them attain their college dreams. For the Class of 2009, he personally worked with 96 families.

Ron Caruthers is an instructor at Palomar and Mira Costa Colleges in San Diego, California, and a regular on KUSI in San Diego's morning news program. He is also the author of several books on college planning, including "What Your Guidance Counselor Isn't Telling You".

He is also a co-author of a book with marketing expert Dan Kennedy called 'Wealth Attraction Secrets for Entrepreneurs' that was released in January 2006. He is highly sought after as a speaker for private groups, and teaches classes on the college process regularly throughout Southern California.

He lives in Carlsbad, and is the father of three children Jessika, Brennan and Lexi.

www.CollegePlanningSpecialists.com

ABOUT ED SANDERSON:

Ed Sanderson has been in the college planning field for seven years. He currently holds the position of COO with CollegePlanningSpecialists.com. His primary focus is to make sure that families successfully navigate the admission, application and financial aid process. With the firm's experience successfully helping more than 2,200 families through the extremely emotional journey of planning for careers, majors and colleges, as well as working with each family to determine a strategic plan for paying for college without compromising their long term retirement plans-- Ed Sanderson and the team at College Planning Specialists are now poised to share their knowledge with families all over the country.

Ed was born in the inner city of Boston. At an early age his parents appreciated the importance of education and moved him and his four siblings to a safer suburb outside of the city. With a lot of hard work, Ed was accepted at Northeastern University. However, after discovering that his family did not have the resources to help him attend college, Ed felt that no one (including his guidance counselor) completely understood how the financial aid system could have let him attend. Disappointed, he made his way to southern California to start his own family.

Determined not to let the same misfortune befall his children, Ed set out to understand the intricacies of the admission process along with dissecting the convoluted financial aid formula. Today, Ed uses his knowledge to educate the families of north San Diego County, where he lives with his wife of seventeen years, Arlene, and his three children: Grant, Sierra, and Brock.

www.CollegePlanningSpecialists.com

HOLY SHIFT

by Tyrell Gray

I n his 1931 treatise on evolution, Charles Darwin remarked. "It is not the strongest of the species that survives, nor the most intelligent. It is the one that is the most adaptable to change." Over the last year and a half, the United States has seen one of the largest recessions to ever plague its economic lifestyle. And like Mr. Darwin said, it is only those businesses and entrepreneurs who shift their business models and adapt to new environments that will survive.

The smooth, easy ride is over. Thus I would like to underline a principle that my father introduced to me at an early age, a principle that many have lost sight of in these days of blithely running a business with an attitude of complacency: the most determined and successful individuals are the ones who seek after their desires with holy zeal. Wars have been fought, lives lost, nations destroyed all because of religious convictions, often termed "holy wars." The reason that these zealots were so determined was because of an inner belief – a holy belief – that has overwhelming control of every waking thought and emotion.

As a business owner, it is vital that you have the same holy conviction about the success of your business. A perfect example is that of my grandfather's cousin, Hans. He owned a small tractor dealership in a small and unassuming town in southeastern Utah. The brand of tractors he sold were not common and had little if any help from the corporate office in the way of advertisement. However, Hans was able to not only thrive in the tractor business, but to be the number one salesman in the state. People would travel the entire length of the state, passing multiple tractor dealerships in the process to buy from Hans. When I asked Hans the secret to his success he said, "You have to believe that your product is better than any other product on the market. When you believe that you are unstoppable." You need to know beyond a shadow of a doubt that you are on the right path; and that if the path changes, you have to adapt to the circumstances or be left behind. Once you have established this firm belief in your product/service there is only one step left, you have to endure to the end.

Finish the Race

Late one winter my father took me to a biathlon with my two brothers. In our area you were not able to compete in the event until you were thirteen years old. I had anxiously watched each year as my older brother participated and could not wait for the day that I, too, would compete.

The event started at the top of the Manti LaSalle mountain range at approximately eight thousand feet in elevation. The racecourse was mostly downhill and consisted of four one-mile ski paths interspersed with three target ranges. Athletes would leave the starting line, quickly dipping in to the forest, gliding through the slumbering pines like brightly colored birds bringing life to the quiet of dead winter. At each target range the contestants would fire five shots at targets ranging from twenty to forty yards. For each shot they missed they had to complete a lap around a penalty course, effectively slowing down their progress and adding to their overall time.

I trained diligently on my father's farm in hopes of not only placing but also coming home with the first-place trophy. My father would coach me and help point out areas where I could perfect my technique in shooting and skiing. He helped me to learn the intricacies of cross-country skiing so that I could be as efficient as possible, covering as much ground as I could while saving as much energy as possible, so that I could be quick and yet have the energy to complete the race.

On the morning of one event, the sky was overcast with a slight snowfall; small, intermittent flakes fell quickly to the ground, sticking to my clothing and impeding my view of the course. I felt the same anxiety that I always feel before any competition, my stomach betraying what I felt was a calm exterior by flopping around like a jumping bean.

The organizers split the groups into age categories and let the older participants start first. This gave the advantage to the younger participants; we would be able to ski across snow that had been compacted by the weight and numbers of our larger and older counterparts. With growing excitement I watched as each group started and disappeared down the course and out of sight. When it was finally my turn, I slipped up to the line and edged my way to the front of the pack. At the shot of the starter's pistol, I leaned into the wind and quickly skated to the first downhill, straining against the snow and hoping my training would propel me to a quick finish.

As we reached the first embankment only three people were ahead of me – a great start, I thought. We slid down the hills and began dipping in and out of the conifers and deciduous trees, going from sheltered protection of the pines to the open and airy quakes now devoid of leaves. By the first shooting range I had been able to pass one more participant and was close on the heels of the next.

At the range I quickly approached the firing line and extricated my rifle from the harness, holding it securely between my shoulder blades. I took a deep breath and squeezed off a shot. Five direct hits later I was out of the range and ahead of another participant. This put me in close proximity to the final competitor – and I was only a quarter of the way through the competition.

As we continued our downward race, I was able to close the gap with the final competitor in front of me and slid into the next range with my ski tips inches from the tail of his skis. Another five perfect shots, and I flew out of the course in the same position I had entered. I knew there was a small meadow after the first turn in the trees and prepared myself to pass in the open area. As we emerged from the trees I shifted to the left, quickened my pace, and slipped past my valiant competitor.

Unfortunately, I was not able to pass as quickly as I would have liked and was barely able to pass him before the trail narrowed and dove back into the forest. Because I was carrying so much speed, I came down a small incline much faster than I had planned. At the bottom of the incline the trail dipped hard to the right. I leaned hard into the skis in an effort to make the corner and made a small jump with all my weight coming down on my right ski. The added weight and force was more than my old skis could handle, and with a sharp crack I was thrown sideways into the undergrowth with snow cascading over me.

My right ski had cracked under the weight and was now completely useless. I was just past the halfway point, and suddenly the success I sought seemed to have disappeared from my grasp. I had suffered what I felt was a catastrophe. Emotions flooded to the surface: all my effort was wasted; the race was over. But as I lay there I remembered my dad telling me that there is always a solution if you are willing to chase it with a holy determination.

Two choices lay before me: quit, or shift my approach and continue on the race. I removed the remaining good ski, propped it up next to its now useless partner, and started running down the ski track. My legs made posthole marks as my feet punched into the snow eight to twelve inches with each step. Needles to say, I was not exactly quick or efficient, but I was able to complete the race. Although I finished last, I finished.

Be Careful What You Wish For

As businesspeople we have suffered a catastrophe of outstanding proportions, and the agents that were propelling us forward have literally broken. It is now up to us to shift our model, change our marketing, open our minds to concepts we may have shunned in the past, and implement holy zeal. No matter the obstacle, there is a solution; we just have to find it.

The biggest shift that I have personally seen is the overwhelming change in marketing. The days of simple advertisements are gone, and the Internet age of marketing is upon us, a clear and obvious shift in the way we present our products to potential clients. People's lives have begun to revolve around social outlets such as Facebook, My Space, and Twitter.

I had the chance to overhear two businessmen on a flight recently; one remarked, "I would not be caught dead promoting my company or my products on Twitter; I would rather not have a business."

I could not help but thinking, *your wish is about to come true*. Remember, you either adapt or you get left behind. It's time to shift your marketing away from traditional standards and think of new and exciting ways to

49

promote your company. Be creative, and you will be successful.

One of the most creative marketers among us actually contacted a local pastor in a location where we had several properties for sale and paid him to promote our properties in his Sunday sermon. The sermon and the marketing only converted one individual, the pastor himself. By the end of the sermon he had decided that he would purchase the homes himself and rent them back to members of his congregation.

I have never seen a better example of creative marketing that produces amazing results. The pastor continues to buy properties, and we continue to expand our marketing avenues. It is better to be the leader even if you make a few wrong turns, because it is easy to shift your direction and keep progressing instead of getting lost in the back.

ABOUT TYRELL GRAY:

Tyrell Gray graduated from Utah State University with dual Bachelors Degrees in Economics and Business Finance. Once he graduated he managed his first business, a flooring business. Tyrell and his partner took it from a startup company to a thriving company bringing in over $550,000 in sales annually, due to marketing, innovative business ideas, and capturing market share through great products at low prices.

Tyrell then moved in to the financial arena working for a branch of HSBC - the third largest bank in the world. As one of its account executives he quickly rose through the ranks and realized his affinity for real estate finance. He was recruited from HSBC to manage a local mortgage company, closing over $3,000,000 in real estate in his first year. Tyrell was again recruited to appear as a guest speaker and expert explaining the intricacies of real estate and the mortgage industry by several local mortgage, seminar and financial companies.

Tyrell moved into real estate full time in 2003 by building custom homes and developing properties during the real estate boom experienced across the United States, which he continues to do to this day. It was during this period that he became associated with Brad Hess, a friend from High School, and began investing in the rapidly growing area of distressed properties in the Fall of 2007. During that time they developed a business system and were able to purchase over $150,000,000 in REO properties in a two-year period. Tyrell continues to use this business model to help investors and local residents stabilize the foreclosure market and provide solid returns for investors.

www.JunkHouseRiches.com

OVERWHELMING DESIRE: DIFFERENTIATING YOUR BUSINESS IN THE MINDS OF YOUR CUSTOMERS

by Jim Parrish

In this era of mass competition and everybody trying to look like everybody else, you must be different from your competition in order to succeed. Otherwise, you give your potential client pool no compelling reason to use your services or buy your products.

Have you ever noticed how all of the new shopping centers, restaurants, gas stations, etc., in one state look just like the ones in another? After all, there's nothing very different about the vast majority of gas stations. Prices are pretty much the same, most are right off the road, most have a convenience store, etc. If you're like me, you just go to the first place you see once you notice that your tank is low.

So, as you are creating, or re-creating, your business, you need to come up with ways to differentiate yourself from the other folks in your field. Create an overwhelming desire within people for what you offer! I have used this theory in my personal injury law practice. In nearly every personal injury case, the injured person faces off against one or more huge insurance companies in order to obtain compensation for their ailments. I have chosen to highlight the fact that I formerly worked *for* insurance companies for a number of years and know them from the inside out. In fact, I have deemed myself to be the "insurance insider" and focus the vast majority of my marketing activities around this *persona*.

I'm sending the message to potential clients that I am unique because I know the way insurance companies function and so I will not allow my clients to be subject to the normal insurance tricks of the trade. I don't use the standard personal injury lawyer *shtick*, which usually involves a phrase like "I care about you and there will not be a fee unless there is a recovery." My point of differentiation is that I want to use my inside information to *your* benefit against those companies in your claim. See the difference?

As you begin working on your differentiating business description and message, you need to develop the information that will help you answer a question that you will inevitably receive from a potential client: *What makes you different from the rest of the lawyers (doctors, contractors, etc.) out there? Why should I use you instead of Joe the lawyer down the street?*

Here's another example: a good friend of mine, who is a very successful criminal defense lawyer, emphasizes the fact that he used to be a private investigator. He uses this background to sell himself to clients by highlighting his investigative skills and experience. It doesn't matter that he worked as a private investigator for only a short period of time; it simply matters that he did it and is now able to draw attention to a special skill that separates him from the rest of the lawyer market.

Another DWI lawyer that I know highlights the fact that he has been certified as a breath test operator and actually keeps an Intoxilyzer (breath test machine) in his office for his DWI clients to see as they meet with him.

This differentiation process is extremely important and is something that you must work on if you want to market and sell your business to its fullest extent. So sit down with a pen and a pad and begin writing the skills that you have which you believe separate you from the rest of your market. Then look around on the Internet for competitors in your field and compare what it is that they are offering to the unique skill set that you have written down. From there, you will be able to see the qualities and skills that distinguish you and make you different, and you will be well on your way to developing your "differentiating" message.

ABOUT JIM PARRISH:

Jim Parrish is a former insurance defense lawyer who now represents injured persons <u>against</u> the insurance industry. He uses the "Inside Information" he learned while working for insurance companies to the advantage of his clients and has recovered millions of dollars in judgments and settlements on their behalf.

Jim Parrish is also the author of *The Virginia Car Accident Guide* and *The Insider's Guide to Dog Bite Claims in Virginia*. Both consumers' guides were written to educate and assist the unfortunate people who have suffered injuries in a car accident or who have been injured due to the fault or negligence of another. These books will help injured persons and their families to understand and avoid the tricks and schemes that are regularly utilized by insurance professionals, which are intended to take advantage of them.

For more information please visit:
www.TheParrishLawFirm.com or call (571) 229 1800.

For more information on Jim Parrish's books, please visit:
www.TheVirginiaDogBiteBook.com and www.TheVirginiaCarAccidentGuide.com.

Jim Parrish is a resident of Gainesville, VA where he happily resides with his wife and 2 children.

Professional Associations and Memberships:

- Member, Prince William County Bar Association

- Member, Fairfax County Bar Association

- Member, Virginia Trial Lawyers Association

- Member, American Association for Justice

Professional Accolades:

- Fairfax Bar Association: Pro Bono Law Firm of the Year

- Board of Directors: Prince William County Court Appointed Special Advocates (CASA)

- Special Guest Lecturer: Fairfax County Criminal Justice Academy (County Sheriff's Office)

- Judge: University of Virginia, School of Law Appellate Argument Competition

Bar Admissions:

- Virginia, 1998

- U.S. District Court Eastern District of Virginia, 1999

- U.S. Court of Appeals 4th Circuit, 2000

- U.S. District Court Western District of Virginia, 2001

www.TheParrishLawFirm.com

HITTING THE TARGET IN THE AGE OF NEW MEDIA

by J.W. Dicks, Esq. & Nick Nanton, Esq.

Akira Mori, president and chief executive officer of Mori Trust Company, Limited, said, "Past success stories are generally not applicable to new situations. We must continually reinvent ourselves, responding to changing times with innovative new business models."

Nothing could ring truer in this New Economy where seemingly every attempt to draw on past success strategies is met with less than stellar performances. The reason for that result is that economic change, while appearing to be the same, is always based on a different set of circumstances than ever before; the flaw is to assume "a recession is a recession just like the last one" and that the results are the same each time. They are not.

Our current economic crisis is the modern-day economic equivalent of the "perfect storm" in which multiple disparate factors collide to create something different, something unexpected, something that doesn't react very well to the old traditional forms of economic stimulus.

The reason for the slow recovery of the economy is because we are not just seeing an economic crisis, we are seeing a fundamental shift in the nature of how business works; and the recovery, when it happens, will not come from the same old stimulus methods but instead will sprout from a more fundamental change of the very nature of business growth. For the economy to return to a healthy status and for business to resume the mode of successful commerce, the consumer must be listened to and catered to like never before. Today's consumers are no longer bound by the offerings of their neighborhood store. What the consumer wants may be thousands of miles away but must be deliverable tomorrow on the buyer's doorstep without the frustration or cost of time and travel.

Jack Welch, chairman and CEO of General Electric between 1981-2001, faced facts when he said, "The Internet is the Viagra of big business." Just like that, the guy who increased GE's market value from $14 billion to more than $410 billion – and was named "Manager of the Century" by Fortune in 1999 – recognized that where he had taken GE in the past was no longer the route for the future.

The reality is, the Internet has changed the fundamental nature of competition and doing business. And although it has teased us for many years with its false promises and failed attempts at success, including its own industry meltdown and economic crash, that fall was just the foundation being laid for what has emerged in what now seems like the blink of an eye. New ways of building and delivering online products and services have emerged and, whether you know it or not, instantly your competition has increased exponentially. Your established competitors are now joined by new companies, fresh innovations and ideas, and ever-improving processes and products.

This is the real crisis that faces most businesses today, and unfortunately most haven't even realized it yet. Instead of trying to rapidly adapt, they are desperately clinging to old ways of running a business that won't work in the New Economy. And it isn't event the issue of bricks and mortar that was the center of cocktail discussions prior to the dot-com crash; it is a case of "best practices" for the industry or sector you are in.

For example, if you are in the haircut business, bricks and mortar will still prevail because you need to physically go to a location to get the service performed. But if there is any opportunity for you to do your business or service in the virtual world, the preference for most consumers will be towards that – unless they can somehow otherwise be enticed by an element of experience or entertainment.

When it comes to reaching consumers today, it's clear that you can't just go on doing "same old, same old" and hope for the best.

The wired world is a universe in constant flux. Bill Gates once called the new Internet era "an environment of constant change" and, more incisively, "punctuated chaos." As all financial players are digitally connected, any downturn or upturn in a major market creates overnight reverberations in other markets. The digital world is demanding that companies react to change, but the good news is that it includes the tools they can use to stay ahead of the curve. The key is connecting your business strategy with a streamlined response.

So how is business to survive? By understanding the fact that as business climates change, the methods of marketing for those businesses are also "upside down" and in need of change if success is what you are after. Where, normally, you would think global economies would mean larger markets, in reality, for small companies, entrepreneurs, and professionals, the opposite is true, because they simply do not have the economic firepower to try and reach everyone or satisfy everybody. In fact, the media has become so fractured it is almost impossible to reach the masses.

Therefore, to be successful in the New Economy, you must think in terms of specialties or niches within broad markets where you can be a *difference maker*. In fact, the more narrow your focus, the more power you can yield within that niche; and based on this fact, your financial leverage can be multiplied.

A Change of Focus

Instead of the reliance on mass media, your focus needs to be on "targeted media." Businesses haven't stopped using traditional media to get the word out, and indeed, it's often an effective launch point for an ad campaign if you can control the cost and monitor your return on investment (ROI). Clearly, however, the gulf between traditional advertising and online advertising has widened over the past few years as audiences fragment and the Web grows to provide a new media approach.

Mass media of the last century offered a relatively simple structure, with large audiences congregated at a few outlets for few kinds of programs. But the Internet provides seemingly infinite choices, and it appears difficult to capture the attention of an individual user when that person has split him or herself among a number of destinations for very brief periods of time. One of the biggest challenges for marketers is understanding this self-fragmentation and how to overcome it.

Reaching the individual who is your target customer first requires your understanding of who your target consumer is, and then your application of market segmentation – the process of pulling apart the entire market as a whole and separating it into manageable, disparate units based on demographics. The market segmentation process includes:

1. Determining the characteristics of your target market, then separating these segments in the market based on these characteristics.

2. Analyzing whether the market segments are large enough to support your product or service. If not, you must return to step one (or review its product to see if it's viable).

3. Once you've chosen a target market that has the size to produce your needed sales levels, you can develop your marketing strategy to target that specific market. Your focus is smaller, but you are reaching the specific buyers you want.

After creating this group of prospects, you must develop your market's buying metrics to learn how many prospects it takes to produce a sale, what your conversion ratio is, and how that affects your bottom line.

Shotgun vs. Specialists

So how does this apply to today's online realities? In the past, advertisers had only one choice – they took the shotgun approach, scattered themselves to every mass media outlet they could afford, and hoped a percentage of those people might pay attention. It was about trying to be all things to all people. It was spending money on local newspaper ads, cable television spots, etc., and hoping potential customers would catch a glimpse of them as they turned the page.

It's the equivalent of the long-ago era of the general practitioner whom everyone would go to no matter what his or her medical condition. Just as patients now go to specialists who can help them treat their specific injuries and illnesses, consumers have become selective about where they go to get their goods and services. Online it looks something like this: health conscious individuals who might have subscribed to a general magazine on health are now signing up for blogs, newsletters, podcasts, user groups, e-mail lists, membership sites, and more to address their exercise regimen, a preventative medicine program that suits their lifestyle, their specific heart condition, their type of diabetes, etc. More and more people are taking advantage of outlets with increasingly specialized information.

With so much out there floating around and vying for consumer attention, today's savvy marketers are likewise getting more specific in order to forge a competitive advantage. They're identifying who their potential customers are, cultivating these relationships, and in many cases even charging them for the privileges of membership. Let's say you have a dance studio in town that offers salsa lessons. In the past, you'd put a medium-size print ad in the local paper, maybe shoot a local TV commercial, and hope for the best. Now, you can create a sizzling, colorful Web site with step-by-step instructions and high-energy videos of those lessons that "students" can pay an online subscription fee to see. Seeing is believing. Even if folks never step into your studio for the real deal, you get them to subscribe to your service to learn how to dance from home.

It can work the same in the sports world. If you give golf lessons in real life, you have to hope people see those local classified ads, right? But if you give golf lessons online and charge a fee to help your students' progress, you've taken the world in your hands without paying any attention to geographical boundaries. You can now teach at any level you want, whether that market exists in your locale or not! Someone might buy an issue of *Car and Driver* for five bucks, but fans who want to go behind the scenes and into the pits of NASCAR can probably find a better outlet, which they're willing to pay more for, to really get them into the action and on the inside of the sport they are ravenous fans of. The list of industries and examples goes on and on!

A lot of these opportunities lend themselves to a virtual delivery with cutting-edge technologies, but some of this ongoing flow of information extends to tangible media as well. There has been a resurgence, for example, of paper newsletters and, although still virtual, teleseminars as well, neither of which are considered new technology. Most of these models of selling information, or ideas, offer the basics for free up front, but if they want what you've got to offer, and you promise to go deeper, they'll be happy to pay for the privilege of regular updates and insider opportunities.

The key to setting the world (or at least your bank account and profit margins) on fire in this world of new media is niche-ing down your market to create value in the people you've niched into. By building your audience, you build your value, and that in turn increases your roster of consumers who will be willing to pay top dollar for the incredible things you offer. Remember – the power is all in the presentation to the right audience.

So, when thinking about growing your business during the current economic shift, think big; but then make sure you think small with regards to what niche you can ultimately serve to prosper the most. After you figure that out, if you take the time to determine the best format or combination of formats to deliver your products and services to your audience, you will find a formula that is wildly profitable!

ABOUT J.W. DICKS, ESQ.:

J.W. Dicks, Esq. is America's foremost authority on Personal Branding for Business Development. He has developed some of the most successful mass media and multi-channel business marketing campaigns in the country and built multi-million dollar businesses on the back of them – to the tune of more than $500,000,000 in sales.

J.W. represents some of the top marketers and professional experts in the world in the growth of their businesses using online and offline business development systems, social media, multi-dimensional marketing, franchising and strategic legal structure to accomplish their goals and capitalize on the assets they create.

A "Best Selling" author with more than 14 published books, and hundreds of articles, J.W. has also been quoted or appeared in Newsweek, The Wall Street Journal, USA Today, NBC, ABC, CBS, and FOX affiliates as well as Entrepreneur's Start-Up Magazine, Forbes.com, CNN.com, and many other national and local media outlets.

In addition to coaching and consulting for clients nationwide, J.W. is also a successful entrepreneur living in the trenches himself. He has built his own businesses, with annual sales exceeding $35 Million, developed real estate in excess of $200 Million and created and sold intellectual property rights for as much as $1.8 Million.

J.W. is a graduate of the University of Florida and George Mason College of Law. He is a member of the American Bar Association, NASD, National Association of Realtors, the Florida Bar and the Virginia Bar.

J.W.'s business address is in Orlando, and his play address is at his beach house where he spends as much time as he can with his wife of 37 years, Linda, and their two Yorkies. His major hobby is fishing… although the fish are rumored to be safe.

JWDicks@DicksNanton.com • 800.980.1626

www.Twitter.com/JWDicks • www.Facebook.com/JWDicks

www.DicksNanton.com

ABOUT NICK NANTON, ESQ.:

Nick Nanton, Esq. is known as "The Celebrity Lawyer" for his role in developing and marketing business and professional experts into Celebrity Experts in their field to help them gain credibility and recognition for their accomplishments.

Nick serves as the Producer of America's PremierExperts® television show, and The Next Big Thing® radio show, both designed to recognize the top Experts in their field and bring their solutions to consumers .

Nick is an award winning songwriter and, the co-author of the best-selling books, Celebrity Branding You!™ and Big Ideas for Your Business. He serves as editor and publisher of Celebrity Press™, a publishing company that produces and releases books by top Celebrity Experts. Nick has been featured in USA Today, The Wall Street Journal, Newsweek, The New York Times, Entrepreneur® Magazine, and has appeared on ABC, NBC, CBS, and Fox television affiliates speaking on subjects ranging from branding, marketing and law, to American Idol.

Nick is a member of the Florida Bar, holds a JD from the University of Florida Levin College of Law, as well as a BSBA in Finance from the University of Florida's prestigious Warrington College of Business. Nick is also a voting member of The National Academy of Recording Arts & Sciences (NARAS, Home to The GRAMMYs) and spends his spare time rooting for the Florida Gators with his wife Kristina, and their two sons, Brock and Bowen.

You can connect with Nick at:

Nick@CelebrityBrandingAgency.com • 800-980-1626

www.Twitter.com/NickNanton • www.Facebook.com/NickNanton

www.DicksNanton.com

IMAGINATION, CREATION, DEDICATION, AND APPRECIATION FOR SUCCESS

by Brad Hess

As a successful real estate investor, business owner, and manager of more than fifty employees; I have come to understand a few core characteristics that appear among self-made millionaires. No one accomplishes and maintains their lifelong goals without these core characteristics. Having a solid base of integrity to fall back on in times of struggle and difficulty is a must. We have all seen 'flash in the pan' success exit as quickly as it entered. Long term success is found once the individual knows how to imagine and create the success, and then possesses the dedication to see it through and the appreciation to thank those that helped them get there.

The four core characteristics are as follows:

1. Imagination

Imagination is where all success starts. If you can't imagine yourself in a better place, getting there will be next to impossible. Everything around us started with a simple imaginative thought; someone imagined it...and now it is so. But imagination is a muscle, and like any muscle it must be put to work in order to grow; if it sits dormant for too long it may even wither and die.

If you want to have something you do not yet possess, whether it is a business you would like to run or a goal you have been trying to accomplish, you must first imagine yourself possessing it. If you can see yourself as if you already have it, you have started the process.

However you must do more than just wish it upon yourself. You must be able to truly visualize your possession of it, feel it, taste it, and be it. This is the part where imagination and simple hope are separated. Just hoping for something is not going to bring it into your life. Hope is easily stopped by the challenges in life. It must be deeper than simply a hope.

Avoid situations and people that are negative in nature, at this point of the process all you need to do is allow your mind to accept the possibility of anything, do not listen to the naysayer, simply allow your imagination to have the freedom to imagine anything you desire.

Have you ever had a dream so vivid that during the first several hours of the day you had a hard time convincing yourself that it was "just a dream"? You just experienced the power of the imagination, which can be so powerful it can even affect our health. Your mind thought it was real, it had a hard time realizing it was just imagined.

Imagination, if implemented correctly, will without fail lead to the creation of the items imagined. It will drive you to start the process needed to create the imagined outcome. You cannot continue imagining and thinking about something without being driven towards its creation.

2. Creation

Just as all life forms evolve, so do you and I. We have a thought, we nurture this thought, and it can drive us to the point where we take action. We simply do nothing – and let our imagination dwindle and die – or we are driven to action where we will continue the creative process.

We first have the desire to accomplish something great; we think about it, we dream of it, we picture ourselves with it. This thought placed in our mind, compliments of our imagination, can be acted upon and once acted upon it can change our entire direction of travel. An individual stuck in a job may imagine himself the owner of a successful business. His imagination leads him to give the idea serious thought. This thought leads to action, and the action results in the creation of a new life.

Hope is where it normally starts - identify the items you hope for and list them on a piece of paper. Once you have listed your hopes, categorize them into a priority. Start with the items that may be able to be accomplished first. Break these items down into action steps and tasks that need to be completed to help the process. Remember that the power of creation plays a role and many steps may not be within your view; leave these alone and let the process take these on. A way will be shown, do not spend a lot of time worrying about the 'how' at this stage. Simply break the desire down into steps that you have control over and then work on the completion of those steps. Allow the creative power to take the missing steps and find a solution.

The creative process broken down is truly quite simple. You imagine something, ponder it, think of it, and work to bring it into existence. You truly are the creator of your own life experience; it's up to you to make it what you would have it be.

Creation, like any other principle or law within this universe, is also influenced by other universal laws. One law in particular is the law of inertia; summarized, an object in motion tends to stay in motion until acted upon by an external force. Hence dedication is needed to keep us moving in the direction of our creative process.

3. Dedication

This, of course, can be the hardest part of this process for some. Staying the course when times are tough, staying positive when others around you are so negative… these are some of the things that derail the average individual, and therefore the average stay just that.

I have heard it said that 90% of businesses fail in the first two years of existence. I have also heard that it's due to financial mismanagement. I 'purpose' that financial mismanagement will always be blamed when the business stops bringing in more than it is spending. However, I also 'purpose' that if dedication were more prevalent on the front lines, financial mismanagement could normally be overcome.

Don't get me wrong. Every business that is going to succeed needs to have a sound financial plan and proper management. But I have been in business where the funds were tight and the sales were slow, and it would have been just as easy to call it quits and name mismanagement of funds the culprit. Instead, I put my head down, dug my heels in, and went to work. Before long the company was doing well again, and I attribute the success to simple dedication and determination.

Dedication is important with any business but especially when the business is struggling. Keeping your eye on the goal and remembering the original thought that brought you to this point to begin with will help you focus on the end result and not get lost in the struggles of the everyday.

4. Appreciation

I have also heard it said, "What you think about and thank about, you bring about." I completely agree. Those individuals with whom I interact and consider to be very successful are continually grateful and appreciative at each point in the process. They see how many places they have been blessed, and they are some of the most giving individuals I know.

I have completely stopped associating with some individuals and groups due to their negative outlook on life. Everything that happens to them is going to be "bad." Whatever can go bad will, therefore it does. I also believe "you're as happy as you want to be," and your attitude towards life can make all the difference.

If we opened our eyes, each and every one of us would find many people in far worse circumstances then we are. Take an inventory of your own life and be thankful for each aspect of it. Truly give thanks for it and physically feel the thoughts of thankfulness. Once you start focusing on what you have and are thankful, then those things you wish you had will fall into place for you.

Appreciation is the final step in helping you reach the goals you have in life; let the goal go and simply be thankful for the accomplishment of it, and the rest will line up for you.

Each of these characteristics is as important as the other, and spending time each day perfecting all of them will dramatically affect your life. To be a truly successful individual with the power to be successful during any economy takes a pure understanding of imagination, creation, dedication, as well as appreciation and the commitment to continually work towards perfecting them.

ABOUT BRAD HESS:

President and Co-Founder of Junk House riches, LLC

Brad started his first company at the age of 21, which included designing a new product, acquiring the investment capital necessary to finance the company's operations, contracting the overseas manufactures of the product and heading up the sales force for the company. After selling that company to an investor, he started his next company, which created enough capital to get him into the real estate business. He spent the next few years working with investors from all over the country. These investors would come to small workshops where Brad and his Partners would teach specifics on how they were investing in real estate. He became interested in the commercial lending aspect of real estate and decided to start his own commercial lending company, Hess Commercial Capital, Inc. Currently Hess Commercial Capital is owned and operated by Brad Hess to manage the holdings and assets for several companies Brad is associated with. Hess Commercial grew very quickly while managing a small commercial mortgage company (Hess Capital, LLC), which closed over $10,000,000 in loans in its first year of operation. Brad now spends his time managing the daily activities of multiple real estate related entities including Go Invest Wisely, International Wealth Builders, Dynamic Financial Solutions, Junk House Riches, DBO Homes, and Pro Financial Services. The combined entities managed by Brad have purchased and sold more that $150,000,000 worth of real estate in the past two years. Brad has participated in the creation of 24 real estate education courses offered from Dynamic Financial Solutions operated by Brad and his partner Tyrell Gray. Brad Hess, in an effort to offer quality opportunities to his ever growing customer base, will continue to expand his interests in different real estate investments and holdings.

For more information on Brad Hess and Junk House Riches, please visit:

www.JunkHouseRiches.com

THE SECRET TO KEEPING YOUR BUSINESS ON TRACK TODAY

by Holly G. Green

The world has changed, and the world of work has certainly changed with it. Everything from the simple "casual Friday" to the incredibly complex, global, linked networks we operate with today, has shifted dramatically in the past two decades. And the rate of change is not going to slow down. In fact, today is probably the least amount of change we are going to face.

After twenty plus years in the corporate world coupled with extensive research in the areas of leadership and management, as well as 'hands on' experience consulting to some of the best companies around the globe, I believe there are six categories of change that tell the story pretty well.

1. Communications

We can instantly connect anytime, anywhere, to almost anyone via our cell phones and PDAs, Skype, the Internet, or even through a Twitter account. Twitter is the fastest growing Social Media in the world with an estimated 30 million users as of May 1, 2009. Each month there will be numerous new entrants in these fields of communications. Blogs and sites like Facebook, which now has more than 200 million users, keep us connected to friends, family, *and* customers. (If Facebook were a country, it would be the tenth largest in the world.)

The number of text messages sent each day exceeds the total population of the Earth. YouTube is not only for the crazy antics of teenagers, it is a business tool featuring thousands of product and instructional videos. Today there are twenty hours of video loaded per minute. And you can be anywhere and even anyone you want to be in virtual worlds like SecondLife.com, where IBM conducts internal meetings and Harvard now offers courses for credit.

2. Information

We are now only one or two clicks away from getting an answer to almost any question we could possibly dream up. There were more than three billion searches performed on Google in January of 2009. Who did we used to ask? The morning paper is now an RSS feed that goes directly to our PDAs so we get the news we want all the time and even get alerts about information important to us individually (like sports scores).

Wikipedia has become the largest reference Web site in the world attracting almost 700 million users in 2008. It is written collaboratively by volunteers from all around the world. Today, there are more than 75,000 active contributors working on more than ten million articles in more than 250 languages.

Blogging has become a way of life for thousands of people. As of December 2008, blog search engine Technorati was tracking more than 150 million blogs. There are more people with blogs today (31 million) than the Internet connection had ten years ago. LinkedIn and Plaxo now have more than 28 million users each connecting us to almost anyone we want to get to, and helping us uncover who works where, doing what.

3. Speed and Size

It required 410 years to invent a photocopier from the mechanical method, but only twenty years to design the modern day computer from the first mainframe. Faster and smaller is a new way of life today as well. Instant sometimes feels too long, and designers and manufacturers of cell phones now face the dilemma that their products have gotten too small. How many of us have a hard time pushing the right buttons on our cell phone?

Distance has been eliminated as a boundary. Teams can work 24/7 across the globe. You're in Paris and you decide to use your credit card. Getting credit approval involves a 46,000-mile journey over phones and computers. In a matter of two seconds everything is done. If there's a minor hiccup in the system, the ten-second delay feels like forever!

4. Technology

ENIAC, commonly thought of as the first modern computer, was built in 1944. It took up more space than an eighteen-wheeler's tractor-trailer, weighed more than seventeen mid-size cars, and consumed 140,000 watts of electricity. Computers are now more affordable and more portable than they have ever been. Computer power is now eight thousand times less expensive than it was thirty years ago.

The average consumer today wears more computing power on their wrists than existed in the entire world before 1961. Look around. Is there anything that has not been significantly impacted by the advances in technology? And who knows what's to come…

5. Competition and Customers

Over one million products are available to the average shopper at a grocery store today. The number of Frito-Lay chip varieties is at about seventy-eight today, up from ten in 1978. Over-the-counter pain reliever choices went from seventeen to 141 in the same timeframe. And your customers might be satisfied with the service you provide, but they still don't return unless the experience met their needs.

The number-one predictor of customer satisfaction today is "Will you refer me to a friend? Do I trust you enough to include you in my network?" This is what drives consumer behavior more and more. Social Media has changed the game of customer satisfaction and trust in brands.

Another key difference in our world today is the elimination of barriers to entry for most businesses and products. The ability to share information instantly around the world, coupled with the ability to access it, easily means that it is less complicated than ever to start a business. Garage start-ups don't appear any different to their customer via the Web than large, brick and mortar structures; and more and more companies are connecting to their customer through Social Media like MySpace and Facebook. Approximately 50% of the video time on YouTube today is for business purposes.

Co-opetition is more common today as businesses, industries, and products overlap. Vendors are also customers are also competitors. We have to constantly examine and re-examine our views of whom we serve and how, as well as constantly adapt to a wide variety of stakeholders.

And customers are not only finding products online, they are turning to the Internet for every aspect of their lives. One out of seven couples married in 2008 met online.

6. Generations and Diversity

The United States has four generations at work for the first time ever, and the differences in the values, needs, wants, and desires of all these people is enormous, providing us almost unending perspectives on every aspect of our business, product, and/or service. Diversity, including race, age, ethnicity, and political and religious beliefs as well as gender is prevalent in most communities and businesses, especially those in the U.S. Meeting the needs, wants, and desires of these diverse consumers is a moment-by-moment challenge.

Expectations and Certainty

Two other things that have a massive impact on managing and leading in our world of work today are *expectations* and *certainty*. There is a lot more of the first and a lot less of the second. Good enough is not even close today. We have an enormous number of choices, lessening tolerance, more self-interest, and a dramatically different definition of customer satisfaction and loyalty.

So what is critical to be a great manager or leader in today's world? You have to *do* the right things. Now more than ever before, the *actions* of leaders and managers are critical. It is less and less what you say and more and more what you do.

You have to have a more complete set of competencies, skills, and traits than ever before. Emotional intelligence (EQ) and IQ are both critical. It is not an either/or proposition. Today it is clearly an 'and/both' equation.

To keep up, a leader and manager today has to *do* well at the following:

(i) Get back to basics when everything around you diverts you into complexity.

Make strategic planning a way of life in your organization. I'm not talking about fancy binders and lengthy, off-site meetings that go round and round in theoretical circles. I'm talking about using some sort of strategic planning framework to drive what you do and where you focus your energies. Answer these key questions:

- Why do we exist (your mission)?

- How will we behave (your values)?

- What is our value to our stakeholders (your value propositions)?

- Where are we going in the next one to three years (your destination)?

- Where will we focus our energies (your strategies)?

Embed ongoing strategic planning in your processes. Constantly check for internal and external forces that may impact *where* you are going, *what* you need to do, and *how* you need to do it. Organize your day around getting to your destination as well as informing, inspiring, and engaging others in getting there.

(ii) Communicate constantly about your strategic planning framework.

Informing is the first step in aligning employees and getting 'buy-in'. It starts with sharing the *why*, *what*, and *how* of your strategic plan. Then discuss and get clear on individual roles in meeting the goals necessary to achieve the plan. Set clear expectations of what excellence looks like, and always expose the *why* behind your decisions. To feel informed, today's employees need clarity on all the elements of your strategic planning framework.

Although the need to communicate has not changed over the years, the tools we use to communicate have. Thanks to the Internet and other new technologies, today's leaders can (and should) communicate in many different ways.

The old standbys – memos, meetings, and newsletters – still have their place, only in most cases these have gone digital. In addition to these tools, today's leaders and managers use e-mail, intranets, and online newsletters to communicate quickly and effectively with employees. They also use blogs, webinars, and video clips to educate and update employees about company goals and objectives.

Companies with geographically dispersed workforces use conference calls and video teleconferencing to simulate face-to-face interactions. And the more tech-savvy companies, especially those with younger workforces, are even using instant messaging and Twitter to stay connected. Whatever technologies you employ, the key is to communicate often in many different ways to ensure that all employees are informed, focused, and aligned.

(iii) Inspire employees by presenting a compelling picture of the future.

Today's employees want to believe that their work is making a difference in the world. To inspire others, share a compelling vision of what tomorrow looks like. Describe how that vision will make the world a better place and improve their lives. Constantly discuss the aspirational components of your model. Why should employees aspire to achieve the goals your organization has set?

Share why *you* believe the destination is compelling. What is it about where the company is going that inspires you? Always communicate with enthusiasm and passion. Become a cheerleader for the organizational goals. Ask employees what the vision means to them. Share their responses via e-mail, intranet, and in company meetings. And share positive customer feedback as well. Give people reasons to feel good about what the company does.

Celebrate the achievement of milestones. We all want to be part of a winning team, so recognize the progress and success along the way to your goals. The ultimate goal is to get employees talking about what the vision, mission, and goals mean to them individually. The more they focus on these areas, the more likely you are to get 'buy-in', alignment, and ongoing progress in the right direction.

(iv) Engage employees continuously by asking about progress and highlighting accomplishments.

Engaged employees bring more than just their bodies to work. They bring their hearts and souls as well as their best thinking. To keep employees engaged, visit with them throughout the year to check on their progress. Make sure all individual goals remain aligned with company goals. Share stories of how teams are aligned and achieving goals. Highlight team accomplishments and link them to the strategy they support. Create an employee pledge wall or flip chart where people can affirm their commitment by listing one thing they will do differently to support the goals. To measure employee understanding, commitment, inspiration, and engagement, take quick surveys following team or company meetings. Solicit questions via e-mail or intranet and address them in open forums. Publicly thank employees for raising the issues.

(v) Build a high performing culture that supports your strategies and brings them to life.

Recent studies indicate that 78% of CEOs globally believe execution is one of their greatest weaknesses. But if you look around and poll employees, it is hard to find someone not working incredibly hard today. Whether they are working on the right things is typically the bigger issue. Consider *what* and *how* you will get to your destination points, and communicate it constantly so that employees work hard on what matters, then measure what matters and what employees can relate to in their jobs every day.

Encourage ownership behaviors in employees by giving them responsibility and authority to get their job done. And then hold them accountable for on-time, on-budget results.

Remain vigilant about reviewing external and internal forces that may impact your strategies. Constantly seek insights from employees closest to customers and vendors about what is going on in the market.

Give people what they need to be successful. When you delegate, clearly define your expectations and/or what excellence looks like. Set yourself and everyone in the organization up for success instead of catching people doing it wrong two weeks after you delegate it.

Review organization processes and systems to be sure they are aligned with where you say you are going. There is nothing worse than talking to employees about how important key objectives, goals, and behaviors are - only to find out your performance management, compensation, or other systems reward different behaviors.

(vi) Provide continuous feedback.

Define excellence up front so employees can set clear targets and goals for themselves. Then consider both values and results when you are assessing others. It should not be OK to get to the end state and leave dead bodies in your wake! There is nothing more draining in an organization than an employee who is operating outside of the company values but rewarded for getting the results anyway. Provide ongoing feedback, both constructive and positive. Deal with problem performers right away.

(vii) Constantly learn and unlearn.

There are almost no jobs left that will remain the same over time, and the demands of leaders and managers are continuing to evolve. Pause and think about the changes in the past year alone. Leaders and managers that are successful today are constantly learning and developing themselves. The problem with successful adults is that our brains are constructed to help us prove ourselves right. And the more successful we are, the more energy we spend on doing this. Based on all the change around us, the things that served us well last year, or even last week, might not be the best approach anymore.

This is one of the more difficult concepts for successful adults to grasp and act on. We get stuck pretty quickly especially when we are successful. After all, our previous behaviors served us well and got us to where we are today. The problem is, everything else is changing, and our *'thought bubbles'* need to change as well.

Thought bubbles are assumptions, deeply held beliefs, or biases that hold us back and prevent us from adapting to today's constantly changing climate. We are all moving so fast that we are not pausing to think and consider whether the way we have always done it is the way we should continue to do it. Great leaders and managers for today and tomorrow will build in the time to pause and think, to ponder alternatives and options, to continue learning and unlearning, because it is only going to get faster and more complex.

ABOUT HOLLY G. GREEN:

Holly is currently the CEO and Managing Director of THE HUMAN FACTOR, Inc. (www.TheHumanFactor.biz). Ms. Green has more than 20 years of executive level and operations experience in FORTUNE 100, entrepreneurial, and management consulting organizations. She was previously President of The Ken Blanchard Companies, a global consulting and training organization as well as LumMed, Inc. a biotech start up. She has a broad background in strategic planning, organization design and development, process improvement, and leadership assessment and development. She has been responsible for and successfully designed and built the necessary infrastructure in several organizations. Experiences include working as both an internal and an external resource for multinational corporations including The Coca-Cola Company, AT&T, Dell Computer, Bass Hotels & Resorts, QUALCOMM, Expedia, Inc., Celanese, RealNetworks, Inc., Microsoft and Google. Holly is known as someone who gets things done and has led turnarounds as well as hyper growth organizations.

With a proven track record of value-added delivery and as a sought-after speaker and consultant, she has received national recognition. Holly conducts more than 50 workshops annually for Vistage, the worlds' largest CEO membership organization. She was recently awarded her second speaker of the year award. She is also a frequent keynote speaker for numerous corporate and professional associations. Her recently published book, *More Than A Minute: How To Be An Effective Leader & Manager In Today's Changing World* (Career Press, September 2008, www.MoreThanaMinute.com) lends voice to her corporate experience and goes beyond the theory of leading and managing by providing practical action oriented information to those aspiring for greatness in business. Holly also recently co-founded the Management Development Institute, offering a comprehensive certificate program in management.

Holly graduated Summa cum laude with her Bachelors degree in behavioral sciences, and with Distinction with her Master of Science degree in organization development from American University in Washington, D.C. She also has her Senior Professional Human Resources (SPHR), Change Management and Total Quality Management certifications. She is currently on the staff at Webster University and teaches courses in the graduate program. Holly also teaches for the University of California San Diego, Rady School of Management in the executive education program and at the University of San Diego in the Leading Strategically program.

Holly is a board member of Total Training, Inc. and serves on the Speaker Advisory Board for Vistage International. She is a member of the Corporate Director's Forum and has served in numerous company and not-for-profit organizations. She is an active member of the Chairmen's Roundtable, a nonprofit organization of senior executives providing pro bono strategic advice to mid-sized businesses and serves as a mentor in California State University's Center for Leadership and Mentoring.

For more information about Holly G. Green, please visit:

www.TheHumanFactor.biz or www.MoreThanaMInute.com

THE MORE THE MIGHTIER: STRATEGIC PARTNERS ENSURE SUCCESS!

by Madeline Ross

There's nothing like an economic meltdown to make a businessperson feel very alone.

I'm sure there are many of you out there who felt like there was nowhere to turn when things looked bleakest. Well, that's probably your fear talking. I know as a CEO, I can certainly get grabbed by fear, but that is precisely when I turn and face it – and invent my way through it! Perhaps this is your response, too.

As a result, I found business partnerships or alliances that made sense for both companies by strengthening and repositioning the two in different ways that make sense for this new business environment.

Luckily, we've been more than fortunate with our SuperSlow Zone® franchises as well as our corporate program, SuperSlow Zone FitWell®, during the economic twists and turns of the past year or so. Our franchisees are still doing well, we're picking up new single and multi units, and we're not just maintaining, we're *growing* through these troubled times.

Why? Principally because our core product is a good value to consumers. Our SuperSlow® strength training is so critical to our clients' minds, physiques, and overall good feeling that our franchisees are not seeing a drop-off because the value of what we offer is incredibly strong. Our franchisees *are* making a concerted effort, by increasing best practices, to ensure fabulous client results and experiences each and every time they work out. We offer consumers an affordable, quick, and effective way to keep in shape and maintain the best possible fitness and health with minimum time commitment and maximum convenience.

So maintaining our market share at SuperSlow Zone® has been, by design, focus and effort. As the economy has shifted, however, so have we – by putting in place some strategic alliances that have helped us continue to grow, despite the slowdown and tight credit conditions currently plaguing us all. These alliances have helped us "swim upstream" against difficult business conditions to help us increase market share and thrive.

Our Franchise Partnerships

On the franchise side, we partnered with the Capital Idea Group (www.capitalideagroup.info), because they offer SuperSlow Zone® three "pillars of service" that add strategic value to our company.

1. They offer capitalization to our franchisee candidates if they qualify. With credit from banks being extremely tight, this is an essential aspect to continuing our franchise expansion.

2. They assist us in making franchise sales and playing matchmaker for us with interested entrepreneurs.

3. They are extremely aggressive in marketing the companies they represent.

All three pillars create a high degree of added value for us at a time when every company could use it. Capital Idea Group solves big potential problems in advance and enables us to increase revenues. Plus, their *direct response company* services several big companies such as Amazon, Universal Studios, Darden Restaurants, Barron's, Sears, and Marriot. Many of the franchises they have worked with have become top sellers. And the fact that they help franchises and non-franchises is important: the cross-pollination is invaluable. This is a partnership that's a no-brainer on our side.

On the other side of things, how does it benefit Capital Idea Group to be in business with us? Because of what I said at the beginning of this chapter: SuperSlow Zone® franchises are relatively "recession-proof," and our company is doing well when so many others aren't – plus we're a proven success story, making us attractive to potential investors. It's a win-win situation for Capital Idea Group and for us. And that's what any business partnership should be.

While it's beneficial to create partnerships within your current market, don't discount the idea of exploring brand-new segments in which to expand your business. Another way we've expanded our sales in the New Economy is to develop a new market segment, corporate fitness/ wellness...with a whole new twist!

Corporate Wellness: Not Very Healthy

The other side of our SuperSlow Zone® business development is corporate fitness/wellness: SuperSlow Zone FitWell®. SuperSlow Zone FitWell® works with companies in three ways:

1. We can set up an on-site, clinically controlled SSZ FitWell® in the workplace.

2. We can set up a modular (if space is a constraint).

3. We can set up a mobile.

And again, here we've entered into a strategic alliance with a powerful partner.

You might wonder what has possessed us to approach this particular market in this economic climate. When you ask senior executives for their thoughts on wellness, they will all say it's vitally important. When you ask them what their plans are on wellness, their answer is to cut costs or to wait and see how the economy goes. When benefits (healthcare being the lions share of benefits) eat up an average of 35 to 40% of payroll costs in this economic climate, you can understand where they're coming from. The National Association of Professional Employer Organizations found that 41.7% of employers reported feeling that health costs are the most serious challenge to their bottom line.

But cutting costs doesn't help their employees improve their wellness, and ultimately it continues to drive up healthcare costs. Employees end up dealing with more catastrophic medical issues that are incredibly costly to the employer, not to mention life threatening to the person who hasn't properly maintained his or her health.

Previous attempted solutions are mostly outright failures. One failed trend involves companies asking employees to provide an invoice from a gym to prove they'd been exercising. By this time, most companies have figured out that compliance with this policy is different than results. They might have paid for the membership, but that doesn't mean their employees actually went and got the workout. And it sure doesn't mean that even if they are exercising, they will achieve results.

Another popular trend at the moment is Wellness Coaching. I understand that type of coaching; I did it for fifteen years all over the world. Our franchise uses coaching as a key method of support and development. But again, the basic problem is attaining *concrete results*. Generally, an employee will be given a health assessment and be put on a plan involving exercise and diet. Then a health professional will call that employee weekly to ask whether they are sticking to the plan. Well, let's face it: there is so much wiggle room here for the employee that it can end up being a joke.

And then there are on-site boot camps. Now the expectation is that overweight people who aren't in the best of shape, or those with minor to major medical issues, can do jumping jacks and push-ups while a trainer acts as a drill sergeant? And we think this will work for everyone?

That's why so many employers are signing on for our SuperSlow Zone FitWell® program. We get tremendous results, because:

1. The employee can do the exercises in the clothes they're wearing to work.

2. It only takes twenty minutes, and it is done on-site at work.

3. It doesn't take away from their free time outside work, which can be hectic and overscheduled, depending on commute time and family activities.

4. Each employee gets one-on-one training to take them to their individual next level of conditioning, and personalized results, in a clinically controlled environment with our IACET accredited, certified SuperSlow® instructor.

5. Each employee is supported in their accountability to themselves; they are able to be proactive in their fitness and health, in the simplest scenario in the world – 'work out' at work! – with no sweat or change of clothing required. And not only that, it actually

helps save companies money! Thanks to our new partner, we're talking new dollars to the bottom line, not potential savings or "budgeted saved dollars."

EEBS, Our Superslow FitWell® Partner

The money-saving element has been made possible by our other important strategic partner: Employer Employee Benefit Solutions Online (www.EEBSonline.com). EEBS has been in the paperless technology benefits segment for years. They help streamline HR benefits for companies by creating paperless systems and other electronic means of communicating the benefits available to employees. EEBS works with companies that have from 150 to an unlimited number of employees and they have an impressive proven track record.

By doing this, EEBS statistically saves companies an average 10% on annual employee benefit costs. For example, they save Florida Rock three million dollars *annually*. Not only that, companies who elect to use EEBS solutions can apply for their "waived fee option." If accepted, this means that they do not pay to deploy the EEBS solution in their company. It's clear that using EEBS can help boost a company's bottom line substantially.

EEBS will also tell SuperSlow FitWell® how many employee workouts they will pay for.

Partnering with EEBS gives me a lot more to "pitch" when I approach a company about putting in a SuperSlow Zone FitWell® in their workplace. I can say, "Using EEBS plus SSZ FitWell equals...."

1. Reduction of annual employee benefits costs: EEBS on average saves companies 10% of their current annual benefits costs (new

dollars, not budgeted saved dollars).

2. The "waived fee" option: EEBS fees may be completely waived to implement their solution.

And not only that, but:

3. EEBS will fund some portion of employee workouts.

4. SuperSlow Zone FitWell® will improve employee health, also bringing down healthcare costs.

5. SuperSlow Zone FitWell® will also improve employee performance. Healthy, active employees work better, have more positive attitudes, and are sick less often.

That's an exciting package to be able to offer any employer – and more exciting with the addition of the EEBS benefits. There's much more of an incentive in tight times to take on the SuperSlow Zone FitWell® program than there would be without it.

Expanding to International Markets

These partnerships have worked so well that SSZ has begun expanding outside of the United States. We look for a country to fit two out of three of the following criteria in order for us to commit to developing SuperSlow Zone® there:

1. Their population is very busy and active.

2. Their economies are doing well despite the worldwide slowdown.

3. Their government or culture mandates a healthy lifestyle.

Those first two are fairly self-explanatory, but the third one may be a little foreign (pun intended!) to those of us accustomed to our American lifestyle. We look for countries where the government officially encourages – or even mandates – a fit population. For example, when you arrive in the airport in Bahrain, you'll see posted signs advocating people to be healthy. In Japan, it's a little more intrusive: laws passed last year require male employees at companies to maintain waists under 33.5 inches, while female employees must have waists under 35.4 inches! Companies in which employees exceed these waistline limits must pay a fine to the government. It has been called the "fat fine." Can you imagine that happening in America? The government would make so much money off fines that the deficit would be wiped out overnight!

In any event, countries like Brazil, India, and many Middle Eastern countries (along with Japan, of course!) meet the two-out-of-three litmus test, and that's where we're making an international push. Our value proposition of the twenty-minute workout twice a week in the clothes you're already wearing, clinically supervised, is the perfect workout solution for these countries.

Use these examples to guide you, and when shift happens, and inevitably it will, you will find powerful complementary partners to help you sell your business more effectively and offer potential clients more 'bang for their buck'. By being proactive and taking control, you avoid being alone and vulnerable when the economic walls close in on you.

There is strength in numbers. And ultimately, this type of strength will help your numbers!

ABOUT MADELINE ROSS:

Founder and CEO
SuperSlow Zone, LLC
407-740-8779
mross@superslowzone.com
www.superslowzone.com

Madeline is the Founder and CEO of SuperSlow Zone, LLC® (SSZ), a distinctive health and exercise franchise. SSZ delivers 'SuperSlow®' strength training, which was created and developed by founder Ken Hutchins out of a $3.2 million osteoporosis study in 1982 at the University of Florida School of Medicine.

SuperSlow® is the original, codified 'twenty minute work out, two times a week'...and you can work out in whatever you are wearing. Positioned as a health and fitness *professional service* (not a gym), clients enjoy the casually elegant environment as they achieve maximum results in minimum time.

The first franchise opened in 2005, now has 38 locations and in 2008 sold their first two Master Licensee territories. SSZ is currently expanding internationally by opening their first location in Sao Paulo, Brazil and working with potential developers for the UK, Japan and India. SSZ is penetrating the corporate fitness/wellness market with SuperSlow Zone FitWell®. Madeline developed a unique corporate wellness business model in which SSZ's strategic business partner, Employer Employee Benefits Solutions (EEBS), will potentially pay for employee's work outs at the companies' on-site, clinically controlled SSZ FitWell® and, additionally, EEBS saves the company on average 10% of their current annual employee benefits cost.

Madeline achieved accreditation of SuperSlow Zone® by the prestigious International Association of Continuing Education and Training (www.iacet.org) July 1, 2005. IACET accredits many of the world's major medical organizations and companies, government organizations and multi-national corporations; examples such as: The American Physical Therapy Association, National Institute of Health, Centers for Disease Control, Duke University Medical Center, Federal Deposit Insurance Corporation (FDIC) Corporate University, GE Healthcare, GE Medical, Mercedes Benz and many others. SSZ achieved and maintains this accreditation to ensure the highest standards of service and care for its clients.

Prior to founding The SuperSlow Zone, Madeline was the CEO of Gylanix Institute, where, over a period of 6 years, she designed and delivered the business systems that are being implemented in all of The SuperSlow Zone franchises. In doing so, she worked closely with Ken Hutchins, founder of the SuperSlow® strength training method, and approximately forty SuperSlow®and non-SuperSlow facilities which served as real-world business and market laboratories for testing and refining all the business systems that constitute a successful franchise.

In addition to her experience in the health and fitness industry, Madeline brings to The SuperSlow Zone more than 15 years experience as an executive coach, entrepreneur, educator, and speaker. She has worked with organizations in the USA, Europe and Latin America where she designed and deployed a systems approach to sales, quality assurance, customer satisfaction, referral stimulation, and internal and external marketing.

Madeline studied leadership, entrepreneurship and innovation with Hecht and Associates in San Jose, California, and completed fives years of study at The Center for the Study of Somatics and Leadership culminating in her certification as a Somatics Coach. She earned a BA at The Colorado College.

GOOD MARKETING IS COMPLEX (AND IT SHOULD BE)

by Benjamin Glass

'm Ben Glass, a practicing personal injury and medical malpractice attorney in Fairfax, Virginia (BenGlassLaw.com). I'm also the founder of Great Legal Marketing, LLC (GreatLegalMarketing. com). I created *The Ultimate Personal Injury Marketing and Practice Building Toolkit.* I have a blog at SoloAndSmallFirmMarketing.com, and I run mastermind and coaching groups for lawyers across the United States and Canada.

As a result, lawyers sometimes visit me at my office to "pick my brain" about marketing. Typically, I'll bring them in and show them all the things I do to get a client. I show them the steps I *force* clients to take before they can meet with me. Then I draw a flow chart of all the things that occur to get a client to raise their hand and say, "I'm interested," and all of the things that happen to them once they do.

Most leave disappointed. They were looking for the magic bullet – the *one* thing they could do to get more clients. The easy thing, the tweak in their Yellow Page ad that will make the phone ring or the quick tips for Internet marketing that will help them dominate Google in their market area. They can't believe that I don't meet with every client who wants a free consultation and that my marketing material dissuades certain clients from even calling for an appointment.

Getting new clients, customers, or patients can be a complex issue, especially in a recession. No matter what your business, there's usually a ton of competition out there. By and large, consumers don't know how to *buy* what it is you are selling, particularly if you sell professional services. For some, ethical rules appear designed to make your entire marketing program look just like your competitor's. Finally, your marketing message competes with three to five thousand other marketing messages each day.

Most business owners, like the lawyers who visit me, look for the simple solution to this complex problem. They add color to their ads or buy huge print ads with their business name and headline; they let graphic artists design the prettiest Web sites that brag about the business, but don't get on the first page of Google and don't entice consumers to *start a conversation with them.*

The problem is: There are no simple solutions for complex problems. There are only complex solutions for complex problems.

A multistep, multimedia marketing system that is complex can help any business to not just survive, but thrive, by serving to:

I. differentiate you from those businesses who rely on the old two-step marketing approach that consists of buying an ad and shouting, "Here I am!"

II. establish you as the wise man/woman at the top of the mountain in your profession/business without your having to say so;

III. ward off those "C" and "D" clients or customers that you hate by clearly defining who you are and who you are looking to work with; and

IV. increase the transaction value of each client, thus *reducing* your work load in order to allow more time for family and other things you *really* like doing, while you make more money.

First, I suggest that you start thinking about marketing in an entirely different way. Shed the belief system that says that you must market to "all comers," meet with everyone, and accept all business that walks in the door. Get over the fear that if you start rejecting people through complex marketing, that you won't have any more clients.

Second, here's how you do it:

1. Start with a different message. Begin by studying the marketing messages of your competition. If you were a personal injury lawyer, you'd likely find that most personal injury advertising uses messages like "Injured? We Care for You" or "25 Years' Combined Experience." A different message would be something like this: "Injured? Before talking to the adjuster, hiring a lawyer, or signing *any* forms, read the new free book about [name your state] personal injury claims written by attorney Jim Smith."

2. Become an author. That's right, write a book. It takes some time, often as long as 90 days, to go from book idea to finished product, but it is well worth it. Have you ever noticed how book authors are respected as experts? Do you think people like Robert Kiyosaki (*Rich Dad, Poor Dad*) or Jack Canfield (*Chicken Soup for the Soul*) waited around for someone to *ask* them or *appoint* them to write a book? What do you think happens when you hand a prospective client a book instead of a business card?

3. Make an audio CD and/or a DVD of information about your

practice/business niche and about your business in particular. Answer questions that you know are running through your prospects' heads. It's easy to create these products. You can either "go solo" or have someone interview you.

4. Teach the prospect how to shop for a [insert your business or profession]. They are the ones doing the shopping, yet 99% of them don't know what they are looking for. If you fail to educate a consumer as to how to find the right person for their need, they may well choose the business or professional who happens to be closest to them, or whose TV ad they saw last night.

5. Prepare a brag book. Yes, go ahead. If you have testimonials, newspaper articles about you, or articles you have written that have appeared in publications, use them. I'm talking about having a nice, thick brag book that you are prepared to mail or hand to people who request more information about your company (because you showed them that an effective way to shop for someone in your line of work is to ask for the book of testimonials, newspaper articles, and publications)!

6. Prepare as many other special reports or booklets as you can think of. You already know the topics, because you know what keeps your customers/clients up at night. You know the questions they have. For example, reports for a personal injury lawyer might include, "How to Deal with Your Doctor: Why a Referral from a Lawyer to a Doctor May be the Kiss of Death to Your Case." A dentist might write on the newest teeth-whitening product. A financial advisor might write about the myths of mutual fund investing.

7. Design a multistep, multimedia response to anyone who, following your directions, reads your public advertising and begins the process of requesting free information from you. In

my case, there are eleven steps that go into action when someone contacts my law firm and the steps *do not begin with,* "Come on in for a free consultation!" The steps include several mailings (real mail, delivered by the mailman) of large packages filled with information, books, CDs and DVDs, and emails that include electronic versions of some of the free reports. Then we call to ask, "Did you get our information?"

Here are the *objections* I hear about implementing and using a complex, multistep, multimedia marketing system:

a. 'It's too slow. If I don't contact the prospect right away, they will go to another company.'

b. 'My clients/customers don't want to read.'

c. 'Even though I'd like to do only large transaction business with customers, I need to do the little jobs for the chance to get the big jobs later on.'

d. 'The little jobs don't take up that much time, and they pay the rent.'

e. 'You do all that for each client/customer? That must be expensive.'

Here are my responses to each:

I Must Deliver an Immediate Response

Do you really want to be viewed in your community as a commodity? Are you really so plain and fungible that if they hire your competitor they will do just as well? People who are just looking for coffee pull into whichever gas station or fast food restaurant appears next on the road. People looking for an experience, *plan* their route to Starbucks. Which is the better customer?

If your fear is that you may miss the big job if you don't make yourself available 24/7, then I've got news for you: *You are already missing jobs.* You don't get all the work in your town right now, do you? Consider this: If you needed non-emergency heart surgery, would you rather go to the doctor who can't see you for six weeks or the one who says, "Come on in. I'm not busy. Let's do the operation today?" Which do you perceive to be a better doctor?

But, Ben, They Won't Read All That Stuff

Those who won't are the same ones who won't take your advice later. The truth is that they *may* not want to read all that stuff, but since no other business is sending them a big package, the very fact that you are doing so makes you unique.

Of course, the reason we include the DVD and the audio CD is precisely because some people will learn by listening, others by watching. The DVD is shot like a TV interview, it even includes commercials (for your business, of course), which reinforce the message that the smartest thing they could ever do is to ask your competitor for his big package of information (which, of course, he doesn't have – it's too complex!).

Preparing all of this educational material gives you a *reason* to keep sending the potential client information. The potential client may be talking to your competition, trying to decide whom to hire, but every few days they are getting another package or e-mail from you.

If I Don't Take Their Little Case, They Won't Call Me for the Larger Case

This objection relies upon a false premise. The premise is that if you do a good job for a client in the little case, they will remember you later. Try this test. Start asking your clients/patients who have had other work done who did that work for them in the past. They won't be able to remember. Merely doing a good job does not make you memorable enough to get a future referral.

The key is that no matter whether you accept or reject their business this time, you stay in front of that prospect *forever* with an interesting monthly newsletter. They will remember you when they or someone in their circle of influence needs a big case professional the next time.

The Small Jobs Aren't a Hassle, and Besides, They Pay the Rent

Really? Have you ever actually tracked the time you and your staff spend on the little cases or low transaction business deals? Let me ask you this: If you have an hour to spend, don't you think it's better spent increasing the value of a $100,000 job by 10% than it is to increase the value of a $10,000 job by 10%? You don't have unlimited time, do you?

A Complex Marketing System Must Be Expensive

It can be. But I often hear that objection from professionals or business owners who are spending money, year after year, in the Yellow Pages, running ads that sit right next to their competitors', and saying the same thing as their competitors.

It is very hard to market without spending *any* money, so the issue becomes, *how will you spend your next marketing dollar?* It's a resource allocation issue.

CONCLUSION

If you are not completely satisfied with the way your practice works for you, then you should be spending the time *up-front* to develop good, consumer-friendly educational materials that establish you as the expert and market to your perfect client/customer. Writing books and reports does take time, but it's time spent once. Your complex marketing system does not need to start with fourteen steps in fourteen days, since you are likely "competing" with business owners and professionals who are doing the traditional two-step *here I am, come on in for a free consultation/widget* system. You can start with a few steps and expand as the quality and transaction value of your jobs get better.

What's great about a complex marketing system is that each time you add a step, you move one step further away from your competition. No, you won't get all of the work, but you aren't getting it now. You don't want *all* of the work in your town because you want to have a life and be a hero to your family. A well-executed, complex marketing system will increase your income with less work. I can't think of anyone who wouldn't rather do business that way.

ABOUT BEN GLASS:

Ben Glass is a practicing personal injury and medical malpractice attorney in Fairfax, Virginia. He is the founder of Great Legal Marketing, a business that is revolutionizing the way lawyers market and build their businesses in order that they can have saner practices, live lives of significance and be heroes to their families. He is a much sought after speaker and has been featured in TRIAL magazine, Wall Street Journal Online and the Washington Post, among others. Ben is the author of seven books, including The Truth About Lawyer Advertising (available on Amazon).

For more information, please visit www.BenGlassLaw.com and www.GreatLegalMarketing.com. You can follow Ben on Facebook at Facebook.com/LiveLifeVeryBig

INFORMATION+AUTOMATION THE RIGHT RECESSION COMBINATION

by Richard Seppala, The ROI Guy™

When times are tough, you have to find new ways to save money and make money. Well, you're in luck, because that's my specialty. When you put together the right marketing information with seamless automation, you're on your way to more effective advertising, more new business, more revenue, and fewer expenses.

And now that I'm done promising you the moon, I'll tell you how I actually deliver it.

In a recession, most business experts will tell you to increase your marketing budget, not cut it back. All well and good – but do these "experts" actually know the meaning of *recession*? It means *nobody has as much money*, which makes it hard to increase the budget of *anything* unless you absolutely have to.

And frankly, I don't believe these experts actually care if your marketing budget increases; what they're really after is making your marketing more *effective*. I'm here to tell you that you can actually cut your marketing budget by up to 50% and still make it more efficient, more powerful, and less work for you and your staff by automating the process from start to finish. Not only that, but you'll also stop losing revenue from potential new sales that you didn't even know were disappearing.

Yes, you can spend less money and *make more* at the same time, all because of three magic letters: "ROI." These letters helped my wife, a dentist, cut her marketing budget in half and achieve dramatically better results at the same time. She doesn't listen to me a lot, but I'm glad she listened this time! If you mind your "ROI," you too will find great improvements in your bottom line. It's a great way to beat the recession.

In case you don't know what "ROI" is all about, it simply means *"return on investment."* An even simpler way of putting that is "are you getting what you pay for?"

That's an essential question to ask – and more importantly, get answers to – in the New Economy. Every dollar counts – hey, every *nickel* counts, and we all want to make sure we're getting the maximum bang for our buck.

Of course, in most cases in your everyday life, you know if you're getting what you pay for. You pay for ten gallons of gas for your car and you get ten gallons of gas. If you take your significant other out for dinner, you pay for two meals and you get two meals. Simple, basic economic transactions.

But when it comes to marketing your business, it's a whole different ballgame – the kind of ballgame where the pitcher and the batter are both usually blindfolded!

It's hard to separate fact from fiction in advertising, especially if you're a small or medium-sized business. Large corporations can afford to spend millions on focus groups and market research to find out what's working and what's not. Smaller business owners, however, do a lot of marketing on blind faith. They may have five or ten different marketing placements active but have no idea which one is generating the most leads. They're reduced to putting the "How did you find out about us?" question on their response or order forms, but most people don't remember, or don't answer. It's not reliable.

That's why I devised an affordable system to track *exactly how many calls* each marketing placement generates. By assigning different toll-free numbers to each placement (my wife, believe it or not, has fifteen of them going!), you can quickly ditch the advertising that's not getting you any customers and, if you want, put more money into the advertising that's delivering.

In any event, you'll be sure you're not throwing your money away on marketing that does you absolutely no good whatsoever. Because you'll know by the phone number which ad brought the lead to you, you'll know which advertising is paying off.

But that's not the end of the ROI story. Or, at least, it shouldn't be.

Because it's one thing to generate those phone calls from potential new customers and clients, but it's another to actually handle those calls correctly.

Small and medium-sized businesses are generally understaffed and overworked. Not a lot of time or attention goes into answering calls from prospects. They generally turn into "data-dropping" conversations. For instance, someone might call my wife's office and ask what her office hours are. The receptionist would simply inform that person what the hours are, and that would be the end of the conversation.

And it would be a massive blown opportunity.

When someone calls, already interested in what your business has to offer, it's the easiest sell in the world. The very least that the person taking the call can do is get the caller's contact info so you can market to that person later. But usually even that doesn't happen.

The step beyond getting that contact info is *engaging the caller*. In the case of the person calling my wife's office, the receptionist should ask what dental treatment the caller requires and mention any specials they have and any other selling points of the dental office.

Doing the above could mean picking up a new customer worth thousands of dollars in the years to come – and I don't have to ask what that could mean to your business. Now, what does it mean to your business that you're *losing* that potential customer because of a badly handled phone call?

One of the services I like to provide is recording those phone calls and reviewing them with my clients. The result? Most business owners are shocked at how many potential customers are given minimal answers at best, and hang up without any meaningful interaction. I try to use these recordings, however, as a positive training device so that those who answer the phones can understand how they're almost *turning away* business rather than inviting it in.

After all, in a small business, sometimes it's the owner who's answering the calls and making a mess of it! I mean, let's face it: in a busy, small office, the person answering the phones may find it hard to give even the minimal attention and time necessary to properly answer an incoming call from an interested prospect.

And that's why I advocate that my clients automate this side of the equation as well. What I'm talking about in terms of answering those incoming calls is pretty simple. Get the contact information, which is most important, and ask follow-up questions. By setting up customized recorded responses to these inquiry phone calls – and adding a "Call to Action" – you eliminate the possibility of these calls being mishandled.

Let's go back to my wife's dental practice. Let's say, in one of her marketing placements, she's advertising a revolutionary new teeth-whitening procedure. A person who sees that ad calls the number we've placed on it. A recorded message offers to send that person free information on the new procedure and the dental practice itself (the "Call to Action") if they leave their contact information.

With our new software package, "The ROI Bridge," we then record their information and message if there is one and automatically transcribe and upload their contact information into the business' CRM (Customer Relationship Management) software.

What advantages does this give the business? Well, (a) a staff member can call the prospect back when they have the time to properly have a conversation, (b) they'll also be prepared to sell the specific service the prospect is calling about, (c) the prospect's contact information is digitally stored and can be automatically used in the next marketing campaign and (d) you don't lose track of a potential new client or customer since everything has been recorded.

Most importantly, you're not at the mercy of having to deal with the call when your office might be at its busiest. You need time and space to really manage sales calls effectively. Automating everything puts those sales calls on your timetable – and, as you know, when you run a small or medium-sized business, time can be more valuable than money!

Not only that, you can cut down or even eliminate staff positions because an all-in-one ROI process like this means you don't need to have people 'inputting' contact information or handling sales calls all day. It all gets done for one low, affordable, monthly charge.

A recession means you're probably losing business. Increasing your marketing ROI means you're maximizing your chances of getting new business, as well as cutting costs. When it comes to recession remedies, I can't think of a better one.

Remember, you don't need to market *more*; you need to market *more effectively.* It's hard to know how to do that when marketing isn't your core business. But it's easy to accomplish even if you're not an advertising whiz, if you just take the time to track your ROI from initial marketing to final phone calls from generated leads. That's what my wife learned, and it boosted her bottom line – not to mention my status at home!

Taking these kinds of ROI tools on board now will definitely help your business short term – and do incredible things for it long term. This recession won't last forever, and when the good times return, you'll be more than ready to take advantage of them by making your business as ROI-friendly as possible *right now.*

ABOUT RICHARD SEPPALA:

Richard Seppala, also known as "The ROI Guy™," is a best-selling author and marketing expert that is regularly sought out by the media for his opinion on marketing campaigns that really work. Richard has been seen on NBC, CBS, ABC and FOX affiliates as well as in The Wall Street Journal, USA Today and Newsweek. Richard is known for constantly asking the question "What is the return on the investment you make for each of your marketing campaigns?" He founded what has now become "The ROI Guy" in 2005, a company that provides advertising tracking for clients nationwide. The ROI Guy™ Tracking System monitors the success or failure of ad campaigns, tracks marketing response rates, determines return on investment (ROI), and identifies the strengths and weaknesses of your marketing and customer service programs throughout your business lifecycle.

Critically acclaimed as "The Holy Grail of Marketing," The ROI Guy™ Tracking System is just that, because there is no easier system that puts the power and ease of real time results for lead generation on autopilot with all of your marketing campaigns.

To learn more about Richard Seppala, The ROI Guy™ and how you can receive the free Special Report "Your Income Explosion Guide: 7 Powerful Reasons Why Your Telephone is the Lifeblood of Your Business," visit www.YourROIGuy.com or call Toll-Free 1-800-647-1909.

www.YourROIGuy.com

EFFECTIVE AND TARGETED WEB MARKETING WORKS!

by Tom Foster

With over two hundred attorneys and other professionals working with Foster Web Marketing to successfully distinguish and market themselves online, we feel confident that we know what we're doing. For some reason, it seems that attorneys, doctors, realtors, and other professionals are particularly vulnerable to Web marketing scams – and we save them from spending *stupid money*. However, Web marketing is an area in which many businesses are ignorant or weak – and when it comes to marketing in this economy, none of us can afford to be either of those things.

Web marketing is a foreign concept that has been largely ignored or mishandled by many firms that come to us. Most of our clients and prospects are looking for some magic bullet or automated method to increase business. They have already spent significant dollars on failed Web sites, directories, and keyword scams. Many of them come to us with baggage. At FWM, we are fortunate to be able to help these people market themselves online in a sincere and ethical way that really distinguishes them from their competition. And if our clients do as we recommend, it is guaranteed to work.

At Foster Web Marketing, we have several different client styles. Some of our clients want to do it all themselves, some of them want us to coach them, and others want it all done for them. No matter what kind of client we have, there are some important questions that we ask them when we first interview them:

- Do you know how many pages from your site are indexed with Google and other search engines?

- How do you currently add content to your site and how often? Can you log in and add something within a matter of minutes, or do you have to exchange e-mails with your Web design company (and probably pay them every time you have this done)?

- Are you doing any link building or using a service for link building?

- Do you know what people are really searching for to find you?

Most of our clients have no clue what these questions even mean, so at Foster Web Marketing, we know we need to educate them *first* about what works.

Search Engine Rankings

The amount of relevant content on a Web site is *the most* important aspect to increasing search engine rankings, visits, and the chances of generating leads online. This also holds true for the amount of high-quality and relevant inbound links to various pages within a Web site. The on-page optimization, the domain age, all of these are important, but nowhere near as important as having informative and relevant content that is being linked to high page-ranked resources.

This important tool is helpful and easy. It's one that everyone should use. Next time you get a chance, go to Google and type this in the search box:

"site:http://www.yoursitedomain.com" (Plug in *your domain*.)

The result will be an index listing of all the Web pages that Google has listed for that domain. You can do this for any domain you want (even your competition).

Why is this important to anyone with a Web site? The more pages of content that you have that are relevant to your services, the better chance you have of obtaining more visitors. This is because:

1. The more content that you add to your Web site, the more authority that Google and other search engines will give to it. They don't care about a regular business site with ten pages that talks about nothing but the business and their services. It's called the *information* super highway for a reason; search engines care about Web sites that bring something to the table.

2. Google can read your entire site *if it is coded or built properly*. Google seriously cares about providing good results for its clients: *Internet searchers*. As a general rule, they will rank a site higher if it has content that people actually read and can use. If you just throw junk on your site and never add anything interesting, why in the world would someone read it and then hire you? Be mindful of what you are adding to your Web site and make sure it is something of informational value.

3. Not everyone searches for the same keywords. The more content you add, the better chances you have of capturing visitors who are searching for variations of different keywords. Are you adding frequently asked questions, knowing that sometimes someone will search for something like: What should I do if I was just in a

car accident? If there was just a big case and someone searched for the names involved to find out if maybe they have a chance at something similar, do you have a blog post up offering your opinion and feedback? Do you offer information regarding your practice areas that are medically related?

Inbound Links

However, this isn't all that needs to be done for a successful Web-based marketing campaign. I wish it were that easy. The other critical process is getting high-quality inbound links to specific and relevant pages of your Web site or blog.

You can find out where your Web site currently stands with inbound links as well. There is another free and easy Google tool that will give you information you need about this very, very important element to your online marketing. Go to a Google search page and type this in:

"link:http://www.yoursitedomain.com" (again, plug in *your domain*.)

The resulting list is all the other Web pages in Google's index that are linked to various pages in your Web site.

Why is this important to you? Pay attention because this is the entire philosophy of search engine optimization (SEO). It is critical to have as many high-quality incoming links to your site pages as you can. This means that your site is being endorsed by other sites that may be more popular than yours. It's very similar to going to a new school and not knowing anyone at all. Everyone ignores you if you do nothing to distinguish yourself. (Coincidentally, this is what most law firms do with their Web sites; they just copy their competition. They did it in the Yellow Pages and now they are doing it on the Web.) But if you become friends with the popular crowd, what starts to happen? If you have interesting things to say, if you're funny or good looking – whatever – the other kids will start to notice, not because of you alone but because of who you know and, more importantly, who knows you and that they think you're great.

Google uses this same analogy to help deliver the best search results for a particular search phrase. It's a simple formula that looks like this:

$$PR(A) = (1-d) + d(PR(t1)/C(t1) + ... + PR(tn)/C(tn))$$

Now that you know the formula, go conquer the world.

Seriously, that formula makes no sense to me either, but it is one of the original Google algorithms used to determine how to get "page rank." I'm a simple guy and not good at math or algebra, so those formulas just scare me. That's why I'm simplifying it for you like I did for myself:

PageOne = Good Content + Good Code + Quality Inbound Links

If you follow that, you will be on Page One for any search phrase you want.

Call to Action

Let's say you have followed all of these rules and are on Page One for everything you can think of and are getting twenty-five thousand visitors a month…

And nobody is buying or even contacting you. Oops.

This is what we call a "conversion issue." It occurs when your content is attracting the right people (or maybe it isn't), but your message or call to action is not appropriate to what you do, not original, or simply nonexistent. This is like Best Buy advertising a TV in their store, but when people come in the store to buy the TV, the store is boring and they really have to look hard to find the TV or find help to purchase it. Consumers will not do that if they can go somewhere else and find an easier way to buy. The same is true of your Web site and why constant testing and improvement needs to take place.

What are you offering that is interesting or is "something someone wants"? Are you offering a product or information that is important enough for someone to be compelled to contact you right away or, at the very least, provide their coveted name and e-mail? There are many ways to market service- or consulting-based businesses (like law firms and dentist offices) via the Web site to encourage sign-ups. You can offer a free consumer report or informative videos explaining complex procedures, or you can, for example, summarize areas of the law for easier consumption. It is only limited by your own imagination.

Of course, implementation of new marketing campaigns online should be a fairly easy process once you have the tools in place to do it. This means you need an online presence that is current, linking, viral, and active.

At FWM, we offer our clients various ways to implement a Web marketing strategy. First, our clients use an online custom-built application called DSS (Dynamic Self-Service) to update the content on their Web site(s). Being able to update your site yourself is the entire foundation and starting point for successful Web marketing.

Second, we provide custom and optimized Wordpress blogs to expand the online presence of our clients. We also provide content writing and updating services to those simply too busy to do it themselves. Thirdly, we help clients establish social marketing Web sites such as Twitter and Facebook. And finally, Foster Web Marketing consults with our clients to improve conversion and the visitor-to-client ratio.

If you're not doing these things, you're already four steps behind the competition. Don't believe me? Check out my reports on www. FosterWebMarketing.com: "Twitter for Attorneys", "5 Reasons You Must Have a Blog NOW", and "The 5 Biggest Mistakes 99% of Lawyers Make with Their Web Sites".

The days when you paid a Web design company a few grand to build a site and have it sit there for two years without making any updates are over. The business who take the initiative to add informative content on a regular basis and properly develop their Web sites are the ones generating the most leads online.

ABOUT TOM FOSTER:

As the founder and owner of Foster Web Marketing, Tom Foster is no stranger to the world of cutting-edge technology.

Tom entered the world of technology initially to focus on sales and marketing in 1991 after serving a six-year tour in The Marines. The USMC is where he learned his initial technology skills while being stationed in Top Secret Military Communications Centers around the world. After dedicated service to his country, Tom's goal was to break into an industry with big growth potential. Retail software was the biggest thing going and large-scale distribution was on the horizon. Tom jumped on the opportunity and was distributing software solutions to retail chains such as Best Buy and CompUSA, where he was able to polish his business and sales skills with executives in the corporate world.

After many successful years in the software technology business, Tom wisely recognized the future of the Internet and decided to go out and start his own web design company. Foster Web Marketing was launched and quickly gained national recognition. The company's websites gained rave reviews from respected legal marketing consultants like Ben Glass, who was so impressed with the company's early work that he personally endorsed Tom and his company's effective web services to other attorneys and professionals.

Since launching in 1998, Foster Web Marketing has evolved from a "one guy in his basement" website design and SEO company to a full-scale web marketing boutique. With over 200 clients and counting, the company currently has a dedicated team of designers, project managers, content writers, sales and customer service associates, and web marketing professionals that work closely with clients on a monthly basis to increase their online exposure and generate leads and cases online. They recently opened a video studio in Fairfax, Virginia in early-2009 - which is fully equipped with a green room and the latest editing and recording equipment to produce web-friendly video solutions.

Tom is also the creator of DSS (Dynamic Self-Service), a powerful and highly effective online application that allows his web clients to update every aspect of their website.

Tom and Foster Web Marketing have quickly established themselves as the leader in professional web marketing services, and remain dedicated to the customer service and superior design qualities that helped set them apart from competitors since the beginning.

To find out more about Foster Web Marketing , Tom Foster, and DSS – visit their website at www.FosterWebMarketing. com or follow Tom at www.Twitter.com/tomfosterweb

DON'T BE A TWIT: TWEET!

by Lindsay Dicks

April 16th is the day after the IRS deadline. The perfect day for something almost monumental but less-than-serious to happen.

In 2009, that was the day popular actor Ashton Kutcher took down CNN, the cable news giant, all by his lonesome.

In case you weren't paying attention, didn't care, or just plain forgot, Kutcher challenged CNN to a race to see who could be the first to gather a million followers on the newest social-network messaging marvel, Twitter.com. And yes, Kutcher prevailed – leaving CNN coming in second and dark horse Britney Spears in third.

Shift definitely happened – and usage of Twitter has continued to explode since then. Celebrities, politicians, companies, and believe it or not, actual normal people, are "tweeting" their lives away. Twitter also won the 2009 Webby Award for "Breakout of the Year." And, checking over at CelebrityTweet.com just this minute, I can see that cycling legend Lance Armstrong just tweeted that he's having dinner with his family (nope, not making that up!).

You might be asking at this point, "Am I reading the latest issue of *WIRED* or a chapter of a book about how to deal with the new economy? What does all this Twitter and Tweeting 'twaddle' have to do with me?"

Well, what if it were a few years ago and I told you that there was a new way to instantly reach your customer base online and through cell phone text messages? And what if I told that it was *absolutely free?*

You would probably say, as fast as you could get the words out, "Where do I sign up?"

Well, that's exactly what Twitter is. Yes, it may be a fad like the Hula Hoop, Rubik's Cube and the Pet Rock, but for now, it's as hot as all of them combined – and it's an amazing marketing tool. All of the new Social Media are, and we use them for our clients at CelebritySites. com, because it makes sense on every possible level.

Recession means marketing is more important than ever – and, at the same time, cash is much harder to find. Using Social Media correctly enables you to market your brand, as well as your latest projects, not only in the most cost-effective way possible, but also in the most cutting-edge way possible.

By using Social Media, you can establish your existing brand, create an entirely new brand, and stay up to date with the latest marketing tools and techniques. Instead of the old school style of getting your name around – hiring a giant PR firm and paying them thousands and thousands of dollars a month – using Social Media provides an incredibly affordable solution with instantaneous and measurable results.

And because most of your target market is spending more and more time on the Internet, it's the most desirable place for you to be. It shows that you're an innovator in step with the times, not behind them. And the sheer multiplicity of sites and tools you can use to market yourself does an incredible job of reinforcing your brand over and over again.

Tweeting and Circular Marketing

Circular Marketing is our preferred method of putting all those online marketing tools together so that our clients will be front and center on the Internet. There are three primary sources of information we post and submit to different sites:

1. Articles – Factual writing about subject matter that is related to our clients' main business and marketing pushes. Example: A tax lawyer might write about changes to the tax code that Congress may have just passed.

2. Blogs – Short, first-person personal observations, opinions, or anecdotes that also usually tie in to clients' main business and marketing pushes. Example: That same tax lawyer might now write about what he *thinks* about that tax code legislation just passed by Congress, rather than writing a nuts-and-bolts article about it.

3. Press Releases – These are third-person announcements of a new service or product that is provided by a client. Example: Our tax lawyer might now have written an eBook or be holding a seminar about the new tax code modifications that will help taxpayers understand what it means to them.

All of the above are posted on the client's web site, but they're also submitted to sites that distribute to additional web sites and Social Media networks. Some of these submission sites charge for their services and some don't, but even if you have to pay, it's usually at most around forty or fifty dollars a month. Compare that with the cost of taking an ad in the newspaper, and you'll see you're still saving a lot of money – and getting a lot more exposure at the same time.

For instance, PitchEngine.com takes press releases to a whole new P.R. 2.0 level. You can create your press release online, embed YouTube videos and wWeb site links, and post it there for free for thirty days.

And this is only the beginning. Once we've generated the content – the content that helps establish our clients as authorities in their field, reinforces their brand, and subtly (or not-so-subtly!) advertises their latest venture – we market that content through, guess what, Twitter.

But we don't stop there. We use an additional application called "TweetDeck" (a free download at TweetDeck.com) that blasts the message we want to put out there to Twitter and Facebook at the same time (it automatically updates your Facebook status as well as Tweets on your Twitter account).

And you know who recommends TweetDeck? The Twitter King himself, Ashton Kutcher.

The important thing about the Tweet we send out is that *it always contains a pivotal keyword.* One of our clients is a commercial lender who specializes in SBA 504 loans, a special government loan program for small businesses. So we make sure that when a tweet goes out from his account, it has the words "SBA 504" or "SBA loan" in the short message.

Why? Because keywords work the same way on Tweets as they do on search engines like Google. Twitter users will search for topics they're interested in to follow up on. If a user is looking for information about SBA 504, they'll search on those keywords. If they come across our client's tweet and think it's interesting, they'll hopefully check out his web site.

That's what all of this circular marketing is targeted to do: drive traffic to our clients' web sites, which have been specially designed to capture visitors' contact information by enticing them to sign up for free special reports and newsletters - that contain more information about the subject matter they were originally interested in. That takes them one step closer to doing business with our clients, and enables our clients to market to them in the future since they retain their contact info.

Here are a few more of our favorite *free* Social Media sites that we use to market and circulate our clients' content:

- Digg (www.digg.com). Digg allows you to share content from the Internet that you find interesting. Once a link and story has been submitted, Digg users can vote on whether it's worth sharing with other users; that vote is known as a "Digg." When you get a large number of "Diggs," your story can end up on the front page.

- Reddit (www.reddit.com). Reddit, similar to Digg, is a social news wWeb site where you can post links to various stories and blogs on different sites. You can then vote to raise the link's ranking or lower it, which decides how prominent the link ends up on Reddit.

- Delicious (www.delicious.com). Delicious is a social bookmarking Web service where users can share sites they like with others.

- Knol (http://knol.google.com/k). Knol is often compared to Wikipedia and is run by Google. This site is more of an article/blog syndication site where users can actually post articles/blogs, called Knols, as opposed to bookmarking the web site page for other visitors to view (like Digg, Reddit and Delicious).

This is only a basic overview of how we use Social Media to drive traffic to our clients' wWeb sites, as well as market their brands. Each client is different and has different needs, and we tailor our services to their specific business.

Rules of the Virtual Cocktail Party

A very important point to note when using Social Media is the fact that the word "Social" is the prime adjective: it's not called "Business Media" or "Marketing Media."

That's why we try to look at Social Media as a virtual cocktail party. Now, obviously, you can do business as well as market yourself at a cocktail party. But you're also obviously not going to immediately walk up to a stranger and say, "Need insurance?" The person is very likely to immediately walk away from you and maintain a certain distance from you for the rest of the evening.

That means you want to Tweet about personal things as well so that if someone does decide to follow your account, or if someone sees your status updates on Facebook through a friend's account, they can get to know you as they would making small talk at a cocktail party. Tweet about your family. Tweet about your kid's T-ball practice. Tweet about the latest episode of *Lost*. And, yes, definitely tweet about your new blog, article, or press release and include the link – but don't *just* do that. Allow a personal connection to develop.

You also want to be a little careful about what you Tweet. Keep in mind that you want to seem professional at the same time you're personal. That means keeping your posts limited to a PG rating and maybe avoiding strong opinions that might alienate potential customers. Yes, you want to get attention, but not the wrong kind of attention!

To sum up, it's clear that the new economy has radically changed things, if not forever, then at least for a long while. The good news, though, continues to be that it's never been more affordable and easier to market yourself to the largest number of people than now, and in the most incredibly effective ways possible.

Using Social Media correctly does take time and effort, but it does pay off in many different and unforeseen ways. Just ask Ashton Kutcher. Google "Kutcher", "CNN", and "Twitter" all together, and you'll be looking at almost one and a half million different results!

ABOUT LINDSAY DICKS
AND CELEBRITYSITES™:

Known as the "Online Celebrity Agent," Lindsay Dicks helps her clients tell their stories in the online world using social media powered websites and multi-channel marketing tools. Being brought up around a family of marketers, but a product of Generation Y, Lindsay naturally gravitated to the new world of online marketing. Lindsay began freelance writing in 2000 and soon after launched her own PR firm that thrived by offering an in-your-face "Guaranteed PR" that was one of the first of its type in the nation.

Lindsay's new media career is centered around her philosophy that "people buy people." Her goal is to help her clients build a relationship with their prospects and customers. Once they do, they learn to trust them as the expert in their field and want to do business with them., Lindsay takes that concept and builds upon it by working with her clients to create online "buzz" about them to convey their business and personal story.. Lindsay's clientele span the entire business map and range from doctors and small business owners to Inc 500 CEOs.

Lindsay is a graduate of the University of Florida with a Bachelors Degree in Marketing. She is the CEO of CelebritySites™, an online marketing company specializing in social media and online personal branding. "The biggest mistake people make online is believing that their web site is just an extension of their business cards and brochures. That approach is not only old fashioned, today it's a waste of time and money. Your website has to be dynamic, grab attention, tell a compelling story and ultimately convert visitors into prospects and finally into customers. If not, that traffic that you've worked so hard to get to your website will move on within 10 seconds, never to be seen again. We help our clients avoid that pitfall to grow their business and their revenue streams."

Lindsay also co-authored a book, "Big Ideas for Your Business," which became a best seller in 2009. She has also been selected as one of America's PremierExperts™ and has been quoted in Newsweek, the Wall Street Journal and USA Today, and has been seen on NBC, ABC, FOX and CBS television affiliates speaking on social media and making more money online.

Lindsay is an avid sports fans dedicated to cheering on the Florida Gators as well as the Tampa Bay Buccaneers.

www.CelebritySites.com

132

THE USE OF ARBITRAGE TO EXPONENTIALLY INCREASE PROFITS IN YOUR BUSINESS

by Bryan Campo

To survive the shift into the New Economy, many business owners are being forced to rethink their marketing, sales, production, fulfillment, and administrative strategies. From my perspective, the businesses that will be best positioned to capitalize on the New Economy will be those who successfully identify arbitrage opportunities within their business models and capitalize on them.

I am an owner of three real estate-related businesses with which I have applied this concept successfully, and as a result I have learned that there are many ways to apply the concept of arbitrage to any business industry. According to Investopedia.com, the financial world defines arbitrage as "the simultaneous purchase and selling of an asset in order to profit from a differential in the price." In other words, a financial spread is being made between purchasing and selling an asset (or *vice versa*). From a business standpoint, these "assets" can take the form of time, money, knowledge, or systems. The rest of this chapter will explore each of these business "assets" as they relate to arbitrage in greater detail using my three real estate-related businesses as case studies.

For quick reference (and a shameless plug), here are the three companies we will discuss throughout the rest of the chapter:

1. **Innomax Solutions** (www.InnomaxRE.com) : A company that leverages several bank-direct and private seller relationships to purchase distressed assets in bulk quantities and resell them to investors. Most of our inventory sells for $10,000 or less per property and appeals to investors who are interested in remodeling, renting, selling, and/or flipping to other investors. At the time of this writing, the principals have collectively sold over 3,000 houses in the last couple of years.

2. **Ultimate Passive Income** (www.UltimatePassiveIncome.com): A scientific, data driven approach to profitably investing in emerging markets. We offer completely remodeled, professionally managed houses to investors with 20+% instant equity (based on conservative, independent third party appraisals), government-insured payments that are guaranteed for the first year, and a one year guarantee on all of the major systems that are addressed during the remodel (i.e. plumbing, electrical, HVAC, and roof). This product appeals to investors looking for a completely "done for you," professionally managed solution for their self-directed retirement accounts or personal portfolios. These properties require a $46,000 to $60,000 total investment (depending on the specific market).

3. **Ultimate Wealth Blueprint** (www.UltimateWealthBlueprint.com): A time-tested, all-encompassing formula for creating, preserving, and redistributing wealth that I have used over the last five years with personally consulting accredited investors and business owners. This information is currently being laid out in ten modules through a series of educational products that will be made available in the near future. This formula teaches people step-by-step:

a) how to identify and eliminate inferior belief systems,

b) how to create a pile of earned income,

c) how to convert earned income into streams of passive and portfolio income,

d) how to structure their tax affairs to minimize self-employment tax while substantially reducing (and in many cases eliminating) federal and state income tax,

e) how to select and implement the appropriate business entities to minimize tax while maximizing legal protection,

f) how to create a powerfully integrated insurance strategy (medical, auto, health, real estate, and life),

g) how to harness the full power of retirement accounts using "the best kept secret" of the wealthy,

h) how to set up the appropriate estate planning vehicles to minimize the estate tax, and

i) how to create a legacy by leading a life of significance.

Time Arbitrage

As a general rule, I will not work on anything that I can pay someone else $10 to $300 per hour to do for me. This frees up my time to work on projects that pay me $1,000+ per hour. Based on the definition of arbitrage presented earlier in the chapter, I am "purchasing" someone else's time at a lower rate to "sell" my time at a higher rate, thereby making a financial spread. Every quarter, when I sit down with my advisory board to discuss strategic direction for the aforementioned three companies, one of the first things we evaluate is whether there are *time arbitrage* opportunities available to capitalize on. In addition, this is one of the first things I will look for with the clients that personally consult with me.

From a strictly economic standpoint, arbitrage should be your guiding factor in determining how many employees you should have in your business. If you can bring on an employee for a rate that allows you to capitalize on a financial spread on that employee's time (factoring in benefits, legal exposure, etc.), then it should be in your best interest to consider expanding your company.

I like to compensate my employees very handsomely when they add direct value to the bottom line of the company. For example, at Innomax Solutions, we have an incredible operations manager who is the glue of our company. She has a strong background in real estate and contract law, and helps us with overseeing our contracts for each purchase. Every contract she oversees creates $600 to $5,000 per property in additional profit for the company. She is paid $30 for every single property that is closed by Innomax Solutions (which adds up since most transactions involve many properties at one time). This form of arbitrage is a win-win for both her as well as the company. I have found that this type of compensation plan helps maintain employee loyalty, while adding considerable value to the company's bottom line.

Key Idea: Look for time arbitrage opportunities in your current business model that will allow your bottom line to grow by capitalizing on a financial spread of someone else's time.

Financial Arbitrage

Financial arbitrage in a business exists when you can utilize money at a lower interest rate to earn a financial spread on that money at a higher interest rate. Economically speaking, I want to evaluate every dollar I personally spend or invest to make sure I am getting the greatest return (or benefit) per dollar spent. If I have opportunities readily available to me to earn a return on capital, whether they are within one of my companies or with an external investment opportunity, I will look at the risk-adjusted return of that opportunity versus the cost of my capital.

For example, in Ultimate Passive Income (www.UltimatePassiveIncome. com), we apply a scientific, data driven approach to real estate investing. We offer completely remodeled and professionally managed properties for $46,000 to $60,000 in emerging markets with equity, rental and remodel guarantees. A conservative pro forma (e.g. income statement) for these properties (with a combined 28% allowance for vacancy, property management, and maintenance) suggest potential government-insured unleveraged (i.e. all cash purchase) returns of 10+% per year. Although my peers have experienced these returns with their personal investments in these emerging markets, we must add the disclaimer that historical returns are not necessarily indicative of future performance. In addition, while Ultimate Passive Income offers equity, remodel, and rental guarantees with every property purchased, we cannot offer guaranteed returns on investment without violating securities laws, so for the sake of this chapter, please use all return projections as illustrative only.

Based on the illustrative projection above, let's assume an ultraconservative, risk-adjusted return of 8% for this discussion. For an investor who has funds sitting in a self-directed IRA that are earning very little interest (or most likely losing money if they are invested in stocks, bonds, or mutual funds at the time of this publication), this would be an ideal arbitrage play. In this sense of arbitrage, the investor is abandoning ("selling") the existing rate of return (or loss) to "purchase"

137

a higher rate of return, thereby making a financial spread. Another form of arbitrage would be if the investor chose to leverage historically low interest rates to utilize home equity, or secured business lines of credit to invest in assets that had a higher "risk-adjusted unleveraged yield."

To bring this concept full circle, look at the Cash Flow Statement within your business. If you don't have one, I highly recommend learning how to read financial statements and running your business by a regular evaluation of your Balance Sheet, Income Statement, and Cash Flow Statement. Your Cash Flow Statement should show where your cash flow is coming from (or going to), whether operations, financing (debt), or investments. Your CPA can help you determine what your cash-on-cash return on your business is. If the "risk-adjusted unleveraged yield" on your business is greater than your cost of capital, then you should be investing your capital into your business and capitalizing on the financial spread. If this yield is less than your cost of capital, you should seek to improve your unleveraged yield by implementing the other forms of arbitrage in this chapter, or finding outside investments to supplement your company's return.

Key Idea: If the "risk-adjusted unleveraged yield" on your business is greater than your cost of capital, then you should be investing your capital into your business and capitalizing on the financial spread. If this yield is less than your cost of capital, you should seek to improve your unleveraged yield by implementing the other forms of arbitrage in this chapter, or finding outside investments to supplement your company's return.

Knowledge Arbitrage

Knowledge arbitrage can take on two forms. One form of knowledge arbitrage is when you leverage other peoples' knowledge to shorten the learning cycles in your business. The easiest way to do this is to develop a <u>Championship Advisory Board</u> that can help you with strategic business decisions. This is the exact reason every Fortune 500 company has a board of directors. Based on the definition presented at the beginning of the chapter, we are abandoning ("selling") our knowledge (or lack thereof) to purchase more valuable knowledge and hopefully capitalizing on the intangible financial spread of protection against frivolous lawsuits, circumvention, costly financial audits, or business-efficiency losses associated with "reinventing the wheel."

Here is an example of a failure to utilize the first form of knowledge arbitrage and its associated financial effect. When a friend of mine established his first unique product source to purchase discounted real estate, his "quick start" personality led him to turn his investors over to his product source, hoping to profit from their transactions. The very first person he turned over to his product source circumvented him, costing him over $16,000 in profit. Unfortunately, there were several others who also decided to circumvent him as well. Had he proactively consulted with a real estate attorney proficient in real estate and contract law to develop the appropriate contracts and systems to prevent circumvention, this would have never happened. These contracts and systems would have cost him less than 25% of the money he lost in the first deal alone!

The second form of knowledge arbitrage forms the basis of The Ultimate Wealth Blueprint (www.UltimateWealthBlueprint.com). It was created as a result of over twenty years of collective research, knowledge, experience, and successes, as well as over $250,000 in seminars and consultation fees with various mentors (e.g. CPAs, attorneys, venture capitalists, investors, etc.). There are various experts we have found who have the knowledge for specific niches within the blueprint. To my knowledge, however, there is no one place to go to learn every aspect of this blueprint. Based on the definition earlier in the chapter, we "purchased" different aspects of this knowledge, realizing that the entire blueprint is worth a lot more than the sum of its parts. Now we have chosen to sell the entire blueprint, which is a tremendous 'value add' for those looking to learn the entire formula under one umbrella by taking advantage of our economies of scale.

To bring this concept full circle, ask yourself the following questions:

1. In your business, are there any hidden or deferred liabilities that you are sitting on because of your unwillingness to have your business model reviewed by a panel of experts (i.e. your advisory board)?

2. Does your business model contain any intellectual property that you can profit from either (a) licensing it to other people or (b) utilizing the proper channels to protect your competitors from using it?

3. Are you the most knowledgeable person in every aspect of your business? If so, could the bottom line of your business be enhanced by outsourcing specific aspects of your business to others who may be more knowledgeable than yourself?

Key Idea: Do not make the mistake of operating your business without the input of wise business counsel. A Championship Advisory Board, if properly leveraged, will be worth its weight in gold to you and your business!

Systems Arbitrage

I was born in a small town outside of Buffalo, New York. My parents got divorced when I was four, and as a result my sister and I lived with our mom and got to see our dad every other weekend. My mom is the hardest working individual I have ever met, and I attribute much of my perseverance to her example. Having no formal college education, she worked between sixty and one hundred hours per week to keep food on the table for us. We lived in a small apartment for most of my childhood in a somewhat shady neighborhood. Our lack of means inspired me to want to do something with my life so that I never had to live paycheck-to-paycheck and could do something to pay my mom back for all of the things she sacrificed to raise us.

The ambition created by my environment growing up led me to go to Carnegie Mellon University for my bachelor's (chemical engineering/ engineering and public policy) and master's (chemical engineering) degrees. I also went to M.I.T. for a professional certification in solid state physics and quantum chemistry. My friends and employees now know me as the "systems guy," and this background explains why I developed a passion for applying a scientific, data driven approach to real estate investing within Ultimate Passive Income. From an engineering-business standpoint, there are very few ways to exponentially increase the profits of your business faster than using *systems arbitrage*.

Systems arbitrage can take on two forms:

1. Developing internal systems that manage people, which results in increased profits from fewer employees needed, better internal quality control (fewer mistakes and less discrepant product), and/or increased customer satisfaction (due to a more uniform product or service which leads to a more predictable buying experience); or

2. Outsourcing one or more aspects of your business to a company who could do a better job than you ever could.

I personally have a passion for the first form mentioned above. However, I am also cognizant of time, financial, and knowledge arbitrage opportunities, and so there are several instances in which the second form of systems arbitrage makes sense. For example, we outsourced our construction and property management divisions for Ultimate Passive Income (www.UltimatePassiveIncome.com) to companies with several years of construction and property management experience respectively within the emerging markets we are focused on.

In addition, one of our lead-generation marketing strategies for Ultimate Passive Income has been completely outsourced to another company. We realize their systems enable them to be more efficient per dollar spent to gather targeted leads for our business than any system we could create internally. Outsourcing our lead-generation system resulted in an immediate 75% reduction in acquisition cost per customer. Once again, based on the definition at the beginning of the chapter, we are choosing to abandon ("sell") any system we could develop in favor of purchasing systems from other companies that can accomplish tasks faster, better, and more efficiently than we could ever develop. This allows us to make a financial spread on other peoples' systems.

To bring this full circle, which aspect(s) of your business is/are operationally weak, or are you not passionate about? Have you considered outsourcing them to other companies? Your advisory board should be able to help you identify which systems or subsystems within your marketing, sales, production, fulfillment, and/or administrative strategies are worth looking into outsourcing.

Key Idea: Outsource all systems that you can make a financial spread through someone else's expertise!

CONCLUSION

In summary, the businesses that will be best positioned to capitalize on the New Economy are those who proactively identify opportunities for time, financial, knowledge, and systems arbitrage within their business models to capture the financial spreads associated with these opportunities. If used properly, these four forms of arbitrage can exponentially increase profits in your business!

If you have any questions or would like to learn more about how to apply arbitrage to your specific business situation, please contact Bryan Campo at Bryan@UltimatePassiveIncome.com.

ABOUT BRYAN CAMPO:

Mr. Campo is a full-time real estate investor, business owner, and personal consultant. Mr. Campo's unique background in engineering, statistics, options trading, real estate, business development, investment tax law, decision analysis, and asset protection led him to identify and capitalize on several investment opportunities throughout the last 11 years that led to his retirement from his engineering career in the spring of 2005. Today, Mr. Campo has an extensive real estate portfolio throughout the United States and owns several companies (www.UltimatePassiveIncome.com, www.RedtecSolutions.com, www.InnomaxRE.com, and www.UltimateWealthBlueprint.com). Mr. Campo sits on the advisory board as an asset manager/tax strategist for several other individuals/companies, and has also been featured as a keynote speaker on a nationally syndicated investment radio talk show, as well as in seminars throughout the country.

Having completed his M.S. (Chemical Engineering) and B.S. (Chemical Engineering/Engineering and Public Policy) degrees from Carnegie Mellon University all within a 4 year time span, Mr. Campo was given the distinction of being the first graduate in Carnegie Mellon's history to accomplish this feat while graduating Summa Cum Laude. In addition, Mr. Campo holds professional certifications in Solid State Physics/Quantum Chemistry from Massachusetts Institute of Technology, a Certified Quality Engineering License from the American Society of Quality, a Statistical Process Control Black Belt designation from Motorola, and a Shainin® Red X® Journeyman designation from Shainin®. Mr. Campo also holds an active real estate license with the state of AZ, and has completed every class in the Certified Commercial Investment Member (CCIM) curriculum, as well as all of the core MBA classes.

Mr. Campo has drawn from his strong technical background to create a scientific, data driven approach to profitable real estate investing (www.UltimatePassiveIncome.com). Ultimate Passive Income was originally created for Mr. Campo's personal consulting clients as a conservative, predictable investment solution in a turbulent economy. Ultimate Passive Income offers completely remodeled, professionally managed properties for $46,000 to $60,000 in the markets best positioned for short term appreciation and maximum government-insured cash flow. Every property purchased comes with a 20+% equity guarantee, a 1 year rental guarantee, and a 1 year warranty on all of the major systems addressed during the remodel (e.g. HVAC, plumbing, electrical, and roof). To learn more on how busy professionals are leveraging Ultimate Passive Income's scientific, data driven approach to secure their retirements, please visit www.UltimatePassiveIncome.com or contact Bryan at info@ UltimatePassiveIncome.com.

www.InnomaxRE.com

www.UltimatePassiveIncome.com

www.RedtecSolutions.com

www.UltimateWealthBlueprint.com

NAVIGATING TURBULENT ECONOMIC TIMES WHILE CONTAINING CASHFLOW AND GROWING REVENUES

 *by* Michael McDevitt

Navigating through unstable economic times can be difficult for just about anyone. There are clever ways to capture inevitable inflation and several ways to capitalize through the ups and downs in any given industry. Shift will happen. Trust me I know, I work in real estate as a mortgage broker. I know you're probably thinking, great, another mortgage guy, right? But while real estate may not relate to your business in any way, the simple concepts I have discovered working in this industry can also be applied to just about any trade.

I know this because top producers in all industries carry very similar traits, and a good deal of top producers within a variety of industries happen to be colleagues of mine. Why do we continue to do well when everyone else is closing shop and when the competition is fierce? Because we know that being in our industry means both good and bad times, so we have to figure out how to keep our revenues afloat during tough times. And the strategies I apply to my business can be applied to yours, now that we're all experiencing *shift*.

#1 - Invest in Yourself

If you happen to be in a competitive line of work, a good way to capture more business is by clearly knowing more than your competition. No matter how old you are, you can set yourself apart in your industry simply by leveraging your knowledge. This is a very simple concept. All the top producers I know consistently increase their knowledge in any given area of service or product they sell. There is always more to learn.

Think about it from this perspective. Don't you feel comfortable doing business with someone who clearly is knowledgeable in his or her particular field of expertise? Add value to your knowledge by becoming more than a salesperson; become a consultant instead. Consulting, as opposed to selling and pitching the benefits of your product or service, is what differentiates you.

Another aspect of investing in yourself involves believing you are the author of your own life. Stay focused and energetic. The top producers and successful business owners I know are not the most intelligent people but the ones with a deep internal conviction. So cast yourself a vision and follow through. *Giving up is the demise of those who have the potential to be great.*

#2 - Time Is Money

My perspective on going to the top in your industry is to work hard via time management, a systematic approach implemented to generating more business and conducting our day-to-day operations. If you manage your time, then you manage your money. Something that is vital in a challenging economic environment.

At the time of this publication, the government has implemented a stimulus plan unveiled as the American Recovery and Reinvestment Act. Although this may offer some relief to business owners, at the end of the day the fate of your business still rests in your hands. I know any external help is welcome, but it's what you do *internally* that will probably make the biggest difference. Always do the math no matter what, and if possible, modify your expenses with minimal impact to your business. Here are some quick tips for business owners to think about when operating in an unstable economy:

(a) *Look at your lease.*– Whether you're moving to new office space or your lease is coming up for renewal, you can always negotiate. Everything is negotiable, so find the most favorable terms. Now may be the time to buy. There are several advantages to owning the space you occupy, and based on the concept of buying low and selling high, well, now is the time - especially with rates at historic lows. Buying now can leverage your wealth more than you know. My firm can help you weigh out those options (fcc@ usfidelitygroup.com). If you are in a position to buy your property, there are several programs designed for business owners.

(b) *Monitor service providers, vendors, and suppliers.* – Listen, everyone is in the same economic boat here. Of course, certain utilities can't be negotiated, but you can and should consistently monitor alternative strategies for decreasing expenses such as cell phone, Internet, and even insurance providers. Ask for more favorable terms and whether you can get discounts for early payment, etc. As a supplier, consider offering more favorable terms to valued customers. You just never know what benefits you might find by looking.

(c) Buy "not necessarily new" equipment.–This obviously depends on your equipment needs, but buying used equipment can potentially save you some serious cash. Leasing also offers a wide range of potential benefits like lower up-front and monthly costs, better cash flow, and tax advantages.

More revenue usually means more sales. For you business owners, here are more ideas to think about to increase your revenue or ramp up more sales:

(d) Partnership. – You may not want to go at it alone. There are several advantages and disadvantages to taking on a partner, but the right partnership offers a range of benefits from helping you reach new audiences, markets, industries, vendors, etc. to giving you options you currently don't have or don't have access to. My advice when in a partnership is to ensure there is a clear and concise understanding of each partner's role.

(e) Up-selling/cross-selling. – Understand that this can come in many forms and it doesn't always involve getting more money from existing clientele. Think about it as a way to find out how to add more value and benefits to your client. Also contemplate on how to systemize your current customers into a constant revenue stream. There may be a way to build a "subscription model" into your business to ensure a more consistent stream of revenue.

(f) Get out there and talk! – This is very easy to do. Social networking,through the Internet especially, has gone to new heights. Social networking sites are a very inexpensive and time-efficient way to network and get your name out there. Not only

are you networking, but it is an easy way to multitask networking and advertising.

#3 - Business Plan Brainstorming

Look at your business model and make sure you have a strategic business plan. Make sure you have a solid plan that brings in your sales. Look at your financial statements; this alone can bring you to new ways of thinking and new ways to do business. Routinely analyzing your financial documents can make all the difference in the world in regards to avoiding unnecessary expenses and assuring necessary transactions.

Make sure you have a solid marketing strategy put in place, as this is the foundation for impacting your sales. Changing your marketing plan may be worrisome, so go out there and get third-party advice from those in your field of work and others that are not. Conducting surveys with your database or existing clientele is not a bad way to get ideas as well.

Make sure you have your management system in place, as most companies don't necessarily think about this. It will not have immediate effect, but implementing and following though with a solid business plan will ensure success. Make sure you have a clear vision as to where you see yourself in the future, short term and long term; contemplate a plan and follow through with it. If you are not seeing the gains you want and have exhausted several avenues, consult with the "right" third party to ensure a clear vision and plan.

In conclusion, there is no shortage of strategies that can help you work through this difficult economy. Go out there and talk to associates, customers, and vendors. *You just never know where ideas will come from!*

ABOUT MICHAEL MCDEVITT:

Michael McDevitt began his career in the Real Estate Finance Industry at the age of 17. Mr. McDevitt worked late nights at Countrywide where he found his passion for real estate and finance. He continued as a top employee at Countrywide throughout college until the age of 21. During his career at Countrywide, Mr. McDevitt was promoted many times in just 4 years and became one of the youngest executives Countrywide has seen. He felt compelled to expand his quest for knowledge in this industry and decided to leave; however, he took his time at Countrywide as an invaluable experience as it set a solid foundation in his career. This foundation was made up of skills that Mr. McDevitt cultivated in every facet of the industry from Portfolio Retention to Correspondent Lending.

Mr. McDevitt then went on to become an Account Executive for a Direct Mortgage Lender and quickly became a top producer in the highly competitive field within six months. Again, feeling trapped in the wholesale industry he decided to pursue a more challenging and lucrative position within the trade. Having experience in Correspondent Lending and now Wholesale Mortgage Banking, Mr. McDevitt then began his career in the Retail Aspect of Mortgage Banking as a Sr. Loan Officer and was educated by the #2 Originator in the Country. Mr. McDevitt found this experience invaluable and was reaping the benefits of hard work and the rewarding finance business. Mr. McDevitt funded over 100 million dollars in loans and generated over 20 million dollars in real estate per year.

In 2006, Mr. McDevitt co-founded A&M Capital Funding Inc. and for two years managed a boutique multi-million dollar brokerage comprised solely of top producers within the real estate field. Since then, he owned other successful businesses and has thrived as a young entrepreneur. Mr. McDevitt's main focus is now Fidelity Financial Group, a full service Real Estate Firm that specializes in residential, commercial, hard money loans. Mr. McDevitt is acting CEO of U.S. Loan Modification Group, which specializes in loss mitigation services. Mr. McDevitt has also accomplished raising millions for many diverse real estate developments and has quietly cemented his reputation as one of the major players in the industry. Residential or commercial, no matter how complicated the terms, Mr. McDevitt has the experience to find the best possible deal. Unlike many in the field, he hasn't always been one to toot his own horn, relying instead on strong word-of-mouth from satisfied clients.

www.USFidelityGroup.com

STOP FINANCIAL MALPRACTICE AND BUILD A FINANCIAL FORTRESS

by Mitch Levin, MD, CWPP, CAPP – the Financial Physician™

The rapid shifts in our dynamic economy, in our tax and legal policies, and in our financial markets pose new and dangerous challenges for business owners and financial investors. However, they also offer tremendous opportunities for the well-prepared. Opportunities to profit and prosper for the long term, opportunities to fulfill goals and dreams – all through new thinking, prudent process, true alignment of interests, complete transparency, and with full disclosure.

Many "money" professionals, such as attorneys, accountants, and financial advisors, lack the time (and their clients rightly lack the desire to pay them) to research a topic that only affects a small proportion of their client base (those that earn over $150,000 per annum, with a net worth in excess of two million dollars), people sometimes identified as the "middle class millionaire." In addition, professional educational systems may not give these issues the attention they deserve, as this is an extremely dynamic, politically charged field with ever-changing

155

rules and regulations. Add into the mix that a thorough analysis of the available options requires substantial mathematical study, investigation, and testing. This makes it difficult to keep up. So, unless you are among the "ultra-wealthy" (net worth in excess of thirty million dollars), your advisors are unlikely to have the resources to provide you with all of the needed tools.

That is the reason to trust someone who is a Certified Wealth Preservation Planner (CWPP^{tm}) and a Certified Asset Protection Planner (CAPP^{tm}). Many of my clients are nice, affluent people, who were furious when they discovered too late the outrageous hidden fees and unnecessary taxes they have to pay, and the excessive risks they are taking. They're bombarded with mixed, or negative, or outright fear-mongering messages. They sometimes wake up in the middle of the night in a cold sweat. These people feel cheated. Is that too strong a word, or can you relate?

Are you worried sick about the market's ups and downs? Are you worried because your future doesn't look so rosy anymore? Are you wondering how to pay for college, retirement, or eliminate your mortgage burden?

Or perhaps you're failing miserably in your investments, trying to pick stocks or time the markets or chase mutual fund track records. No one has the guts to provide a viable alternative, to tell you the truth, to tell you that you're wasting time while losing lots of money. You'd have a better chance at the roulette wheel, and it would be more fun.

That's why my mission is to empower you to achieve financial fulfillment and peace of mind as your "Chief Financial Doctor." Investor by investor, I am stopping the financial malpractice and facilitating the cure for financial cancer. I provide a completely independent financial second opinion to help you progress from scarcity, loss, fear, and frustration to abundance and peace of mind.

Do you ever wonder or worry about whether…

- your personal and/or business assets are properly protected from personal or business predators and creditors?

- there are viable income tax reduction plans that will allow deductions between $25,000-$250,000 per year in addition to a traditional 401(k)/profit sharing plan?

- your estate is properly set up to minimize, defer, or eliminate estate taxes and take care of the family in the event of death?

- your personal finances are invested correctly and whether there are ways to mitigate investment risk/volatility and reduce or defer capital gains on investments, and additionally, if there are ways to mitigate or eliminate capital gains taxes on the sale of appreciated real estate or stocks?

- your businesses are run in the most financially efficient manner?

- you can reach "Critical Capital Mass" (CCM) to achieve Financial Freedom?

No Perfect Plan: Real World Math

Let me first state that there is no "perfect" way to build, protect, preserve, or transfer wealth; nor is there any one plan that is a good fit for everyone (no matter who tells you otherwise). Real world math applied to your specific situation is a necessary component to make an informed decision.

What are your answers to the following questions? (Hint: these are not trick questions.)

1. Are tax-deferred retirement (also known as "qualified") plans tax-hostile or tax-favorable? Most will say that tax-deferred accounts are always tax-favorable. You may be surprised to discover the real truth.

2. Are income tax rates most likely going to be the same in your senior years, and are you most likely going to be in the same income tax bracket? Most of us will acknowledge that income tax rates are at historic lows for modern times and that the chance of them going up significantly is high.

3. From a financial standpoint, is it a good idea to pay down the mortgage on your home? While the answer for most of our readers is no longer a secret, it could be that it is not necessarily a good idea for you to pay down the debt on your home (so long as you have the discipline to use that same money to build wealth elsewhere). This chapter can show you why and how.

4. Does it make sense to remove some of the equity from your home to build a tax-favorable nest egg? Though it seems a bit counterintuitive to incur more debt in an effort to build wealth, for many, removing equity from a home to build wealth may be the single best way to help them build a secure and tax-favorable retirement nest egg.

There are risks we know, risks we know we don't know, and risks we don't know we don't know. Taxation is a risk we know. Taxation is probably the biggest risk you face. For example, you may think that FDIC insured CDs are the safest form of investment. However, as counterintuitive it may be, and however contrary to what some financial media "pundits" have espoused, a simple fixed annuity may turn out to be far safer. Despite its expense.

Let's look at how they may compare on $100,000. First, their rates of return are often very similar. Assume they are equal at 3%. Neither provides upside potential, and both have limited principal guarantees of sorts. Both have early withdrawal penalties. The differences lie mainly in their tax treatment, in creditor protection, and estate planning (in many cases annuities usually lie outside the estate, and often are creditor protected). The CD interest return is counted as income for tax purposes, and is taxed in the year it is applied. Not only is it taxed, but also that income is counted against you for Social Security distributions.

Yes, Social Security represents an insignificant amount for many of you reading this book. But stay with this. For easy figuring, assume also you are in the 33% bracket; with the CD's net growth of 3%, the after-tax yield is $2000. Next year (if it could be reinvested at exactly the same rate) the growth of an additional 3% is on only $102,000. On the other hand, the annuity is not (even partially) taxed until it is distributed, and the next year's 3% return gets to grow on $103,000. Moreover, even when distributions (through annuitization) begin, only the small, taxable portion counts against you for Social Security purposes. So safety needs to be thoroughly analyzed. Things are not always as they seem. Things are not always as they have been taught.

The Third Sure Thing

John Maynard Keynes, the British economist who is venerated by some and abhorred by others, nevertheless was a clever and educated person. He said in the long run, "We are all dead." That is a truism. But how do we measure the long run? For this day and time, I submit it is twenty years or more.

It has been said that there are only two sure things in life – death and taxes. No one can stop or predict your death. And I wrote this chapter specifically to show you how to avoid, defer, eliminate, or reduce your tax burden, through "bright line," legal, safe, and proven strategies. For a discussion on some of the inappropriate offerings that you must avoid, contact me directly via info@levinwealthsystems.com.

So what is the third sure thing in life? Inflation. No one can stop inflation. Not enough inflation is a bad thing. Think deflation and the Depression. Too much may be a worse thing. It destroys wealth and income and results in perverse incentives and behaviors. The "right" amount of inflation seems to be in the 2-3% range. Historically, over the past several centuries, by all measures, in all countries examined, inflation has averaged 3-3.5%. That also has been the average rate of inflation over the past fifty years in the United States.

How does the long run relate to inflation? As an example of inflation, my father recently purchased a Lexus. Not the top-of-the-line model, either. In fact, it was the entry level ES 330. He paid twice as much for that car as he did for his first house. That is inflation's long-term erosion of your purchasing power. That erosion is inevitable. We must plan for inflation and be prepared for it.

It may be urban myth, but someone once calculated that if you took the twenty-four dollars in wampum paid for Manhattan Island four hundred years ago, and invested it at 1.5% over inflation (the documented average long-term rate of return for real estate investments), that investment would now equal the total value of all the real estate on the island. Even if that is untrue, the point is clear: inflation is another major threat to your assets.

Could inflation be the world's eighth deadly evil? Well, inflation is the inverse of compound interest. Albert Einstein called compound interest the eighth wonder of the world. And the above annuity-to-CD comparison demonstrates one simple method to harness compound interest (by deferring taxes) to combat inflation.

<u>It is not how much you make; it is how much you keep.</u>

I am not telling you to be miserly. On the contrary, sharing your bounty with loved ones and via charitable giving is one of the things I believe in and participate in. It is in our culture to be charitable. Imagine how much worse off we would be if the ultra-wealthy did not achieve their wealth, and then did not give it away intelligently. Hospitals, libraries, museums, universities, and concert halls – all are funded by philanthropists who created tremendous wealth and then gave it away.

But charitable giving is not the point. Rather, properly retaining what is rightfully yours, and obtaining and utilizing the smart tools now available can provide you with the freedom to exercise your choices for your wealth in any way you deem appropriate. That freedom, that confidence, and that security is *the point*.

What I *am* saying is that there are numerous and tremendously treacherous traps set by those who apparently have designs to separate you from your wealth – the IRS, trial attorneys, government policy, unscrupulous bankers, unwitting advisors, feckless associates – and are waiting to take what is yours.

If you take nothing else from this chapter, I hope you take away enough motivation to become proactive in developing an appropriate and effective investment policy statement; implementing your investment plan; protecting your assets; trying to save on income, estate, and capital gains taxes; and trying to more efficiently and effectively run your business or your family enterprise when you plan for transitioning your wealth. That motivation, along with fortitude (or help from your coach) can help you to avoid the big mistakes that wind up costing you.

This is the reason why I founded Phipps Lane, LLC, a registered investment advisory firm dedicated to *"empowering investors to build, protect, and preserve their prosperity through their own Financial Fortress."* It is my job to bring you and people like you a process for prudence and prosperity so you can find control, clarity, comfort, and confidence regarding these important subjects. On my Web site, www.levinwealthsystems.com, you can access my seminars and webinars, as well as the books I've written to educate you about your money.

Once you have discovered the secrets to building and maintaining your *Financial Fortress*, you can fulfill your purpose for your money. You can feel independence and dignity through financial freedom. Then, if you choose, and if you have enough, you can be charitable as well. Or not. On your own terms. Financially free, independent, and confident.

ABOUT MITCH LEVIN, MD:

Mitchell Levin, MD, CWPP, CAPP, the Financial Physician™, is a Financial Wealth Coach, founder and CEO of Levin Wealth Systems, LLC (www.LevinWealthSystems. com) and Managing Director of Phipps Lane, LLC, (www. PhippsLane.com) a Registered Investment Advisory firm. He is dedicated to *"empowering investors to achieve Healthy Investment Returns™ and to build, protect, and preserve your prosperity through your own Financial Fortress."*

Dr. Mitch is an "A" rated Florida State Representative of the **Asset Protection Society**, is a member of the **Wealth Preservation Institute**, the **National Association of Professional College Advisors**, **The National Association of College Financial Advisors**, and the **Financial Planning Association**.

Author, speaker, and trusted advisor: Dr. Mitch is the co-author of numerous articles, and several books (**Cover Your Assets; How to Build, Maintain and Protect your Financial Fortress**; **The Lies My Broker Taught Me**; **101 Truths about Money and Investing**; and **Secrets of a Worry Free Retirement**), and has been featured in several educational CD's (**The Seven Deadly Investor Traps, How the Really Smart Money Invests),** and in the **acclaimed documentary movie "Navigating the Fog of Investing"** alongside several **Nobel Prize Laureates**.

In addition, Mitch is certified in Florida to provide Continuing Professional Education credits to Certified Public Accountants. Some of his speaking engagements include, "The Myths of Investing," "College Funding Solutions," "This Time is (Never) Different," "The Affluent Survival Guide," "Why Mutual Funds Stink," "Why Your Insurance Agent is Costing You Tens or Hundreds of Thousands of Dollars," "How to Prosper in the Reign of Error," and "Your Asset Protection is Inadequate."

His clients are nice, affluent, successful people, who actually may be **furious** when they discover -- too late -- the poor outcomes, outrageous and hidden fees, and unnecessary taxes they have to pay. And the excessive risks they're taking – that's another conversation completely. They're bombarded with mixed, or negative, or outright fear-mongering messages; and sometimes wake up in the middle of the night in a cold sweat. These people feel **cheated**.

Some are **worried sick** about the markets ups and downs... and their futures don't look so rosy anymore. They then become concerned with how to pay for college for their kids, how to reach retirement, and how to eliminate their mortgage burden among many other pressures. They're looking for new ideas and don't know who to turn to.

Still others may be having trouble admitting they're **failing miserably** in their investments, trying to pick stocks, or time the markets, or chase mutual fund track records. They would stop, but no one has the guts to provide a viable alternative, to tell them the truth, to tell them they're wasting time while losing lots of money. They'd have a better chance at the roulette wheel, without the fun.

Is any of this familiar to you, or someone you know?

Mitch's mission is to "*Empower investors to achieve financial fulfillment and peace of mind*," as your "Chief Financial Physician™." To help stop the financial malpractice and facilitate the cure for financial cancer. To help you progress from scarcity, losses, fear, and frustration to abundance and peace of mind; Mitch provides a completely independent Financial Second Opinion™.

While in medical school, Mitch was instrumental in setting up the first (and completely student financed) long-term endowment campaign through insurance and derivative products. He was recruited by Orlando Regional Medical Center to open the first full-time eye surgery practice at one of its facilities. The practices grew to several locations with dozens of employees, including several now prominent surgeons. He has lived with his family in Central Florida since 1986 and has been involved professionally in the financial world since 2005.

A small business owner, Mitch has built, grown, bought and sold several other business entities. In addition, he is a successful commercial real estate investor. Dr. Mitch is a major donor to charitable organizations and has served as an officer on several Boards of Trustees. The knowledge he gained through these experiences contributed to his personal financial success and the ability to pursue his passion of educating and assisting others in their quest for financial freedom. Contact: info@levinwealthsystems.com

If you take nothing else from this chapter, we hope you take away enough motivation (if you need it) to become pro-active: when developing an appropriate and effective investment policy statement; when implementing your investment plan; when trying to protect your assets; when trying to save on income, estate, and capital gains taxes; and when trying to more efficiently and effectively run your business, or your family enterprise; when you plan for transitioning your wealth.

That motivation, along with fortitude (or help from your coach), can allow you to avoid the Big Mistakes that wind up costing loads. It is our intention that you will have discovered for yourself the secrets to building and maintaining your financial fortress and that you find it useful to fulfill your purpose for your money. Dr. Mitch will help you find control, clarity, comfort, and confidence. In short, Dr. Mitch will help you achieve independence and dignity, through financial freedom.

www.LevinWealthSystems.com

GETTING PAST DEBT: REGROUP, RESTRUCTURE, REBUILD!

by James Brown

Many people in America shuddered when General Motors, once America's mightiest corporation, filed for Chapter 11 bankruptcy on June 1, 2009. It was the largest industrial company bankruptcy in history. This meant GM could no longer be listed on the Dow Jones Industrial Average – it ended up being replaced in the S&P 500 by DeVry Institute, a nationwide secondary education company.

Many attempts were made to prevent the bankruptcy from happening. Stockholders, investors, and the unions were all pressured to make insane deals to keep GM going as it was. Pundits expounded on how this meant the death of industrial America – and possibly the end of GM.

Forty days later, GM exited bankruptcy protection much sooner than anyone expected. Because of the filing, they were able to shed a lot of massive debt and build a "leaner, meaner" company more appropriate to the times. It's too soon to tell whether they can achieve the mammoth success they once enjoyed, but one thing is for sure: the company, as restructured, has an incredibly higher chance of surviving and thriving

167

because *it was forced to change.*

And it might just be the best thing that ever happened to them.

When the economy shifts, there's no question that *you* have to shift the way you do business. The problem you may be facing as a businessperson, however, is that you might feel you can't continue as a viable company. Your hands are tied with debt, your revenues are down, and you might feel trapped and hopeless, just like our old friend GM was.

But like GM, there are steps you can take if you're willing to face your situation. The good news is that you still have options to not only survive this downturn but also use certain aspects of it to your advantage. No, you won't get the $50 billion in financial assistance they did – but you also probably don't have the $172 billion in debt.

As a bankruptcy lawyer, I've obviously had a lot of firsthand experience helping people through this difficult economic shift. It's my job to give them the tools, advice, and legal expertise to do everything I can to get them back on their feet. There are several common issues among business owners that must be addressed and are easily solved, although they are best avoided altogether.

1. Debt

In the last few months, I have seen more and more small business owners come in carrying a large amount of debt and who are unable to cope with it anymore. They were no different than GM or a lot of other huge companies. They all had this in common: the money was suddenly no longer coming in the door the way it once was, but it was still definitely going *out* the door – and we all know that's a one-way flow no one can sustain.

Not only that, but lenders and banks were suddenly not lending money *at all* for a few months, just when small businesses desperately needed some money to get them through this very rough patch. Some even had established credit lines, which they relied on to survive the ups and downs of normal business operations, simply cut off.

2. Personal Liability

Many of the business owners' companies in trouble had originally structured their business as a Limited Liability Company (LLC), or "S" or "C" Corporations – which is a great thing, but they weren't using that fact to their advantage. You see, each of those business entities have legal protections in place to prevent their owners from being *personally* responsible for most business debt and lawsuits filed against the company (the exception being a sole proprietorship set-up, where that legal protection is not available). Setting up a proper LLC or corporation creates an entity that is legally considered separate from the business owner as a person.

Yet too often, when push came to shove and the business owner was negotiating on behalf of their business for a lease on office space or expensive equipment, or even a line of credit, the other party asked the owner to sign a *personal guarantee* on the debt. And without thinking through the potential consequences, the owner did just that, putting themselves on the line for monies owed. This is similar to being a cosigner on a loan with someone. It negates any protection from having an LLC or corporation, the very legal entity they formed in order to get that kind of protection!

So these business owners ended up on the hook for debts they shouldn't be responsible for, the kind of debts GM was able to renegotiate or make disappear altogether when they worked with the bankruptcy court.

3. Nonpayment of Taxes

Another common downfall to the troubled business owner is the nonpayment of fiduciary taxes. A fiduciary tax is any tax that the business collects on behalf of someone else. For instance, the business collects payroll taxes from an employee and pays it over to the federal and/or state government. The same is true of sales tax collected from customers.

What makes it even worse is that there is a big exception to the debt protection a corporation or LLC provides a business owner – and that is *personal* liability as a result of non-payment of these fiduciary taxes. Payroll tax debt, sales tax debt, etc., do not go away even if the business closes. The fiduciary tax debt passes through to the owner of the business personally. In fact, in some cases, the person at the company responsible for paying those taxes may even be liable, even if they aren't in an ownership position.

Many small business owners will put off paying those taxes until the end of the quarter or until legally required because they are behind on other debt, such as rent or lease payments, and not paying those bills can jeopardize their day-to-day business. When those taxes become due, however, they don't have the money to pay them – and they end up getting hit with high penalties and fines. Once again, they put themselves in danger of being forced to personally pay those fines, penalties, and actual underlying taxes if the company does end up going under.

Even if the company declares bankruptcy, it won't help the owner very much. Owners are left with the heavy tax debt and fines, as well as the responsibility for whatever debt for which they signed personal guarantees. In that case, there usually isn't much choice but to file for personal bankruptcy. And even then, there is no guarantee that any fiduciary taxes owed will be eliminated.

Preemption and Problem-solving

There are ways to avoid these common pitfalls. Build your business realistically, slow and steady. Avoid as much debt as you can, and avoid signing personal guarantees for loans. There may be instances in which it is difficult not to sign those kinds of guarantees, especially if your business is not well established. Banks and lending institutions, of course, are extremely difficult to get credit from these days, but do the best you can.

Also, try to pay your business taxes on a timely basis. Renegotiate your other debt if you are falling behind. This is an excellent time to do just that. Most companies that are owed money are terrified they won't get *anything* paid back in this tight economy, so you might be surprised at your bargaining power in this situation. I've found that paying back twenty-five cents on the dollar is not at all unusual in this climate.

Take advantage of that fact and make the best deal you can if you're struggling. It's not in anyone's interests – yours or theirs – if your company ends up going under. In addition, a personal guarantee means nothing if a business owner ends up filing for personal bankruptcy protection. Landlords and other creditors are increasingly coming up with creative ways to help manage your debt for you; don't be afraid to ask for what you need.

If you manage everything correctly, you'll be surprised at how much you can survive. I had one client who ran a "Chocolate Café" – a little place where you could have coffee, a sweet treat, and use the free Wi-

Fi service provided. It was set up as a corporation, which afforded her the protections mentioned above. Her business was actually doing very well; she had a regular, reliable clientele, and it was building.

The problem was that she also had a huge debt load that she'd incurred to grow the business fast that was threatening her survival. As with many people, she did not pay employment and sales tax so she would be able to pay for rent, supplies, and the utilities needed to keep customers coming. She was so far in the hole that she couldn't make a profit. She truly thought she had no options.

I helped her develop a plan to pay off her outstanding fiduciary taxes with the money she had available. Once that was done, I had advised her to dissolve her current corporation and do what's termed "winding up" the company affairs, which is required by most state laws.

Since the corporation held most of her remaining debt, it went away when the company was shut down – the creditors were informed that the company was ceasing business. She then reincorporated as a new entity and was able to continue operating her café. Sound familiar? It's pretty close to what General Motors did inside its bankruptcy case!

And it's not that complicated. Let's say she was doing business as "The Jones Chocolate and Coffee Company." She could legally dissolve the first entity under state law and reincorporate as "The Jones Coffee and Chocolate Company" and go on as before, but without the crippling debt that would have eventually put her out of business.

Obviously, before you start this process, you have to negotiate with your landlord to keep your business in the same space. But it can be done if you've built the business properly and effectively used the protections that are afforded by your corporate entity. Above all else, the first step you should take before trying any of this yourself is to consult with an attorney experienced in corporate law, debt structuring, and bankruptcy relief.

Again, if all else fails, and you do find your company unable to continue – and yourself personally liable for a staggering amount of debt – you still have consumer bankruptcy as a final option. And it is an option, despite what you might have heard about the laws changing back in 2005. The protections are still there for people facing a potential lifetime of struggle with no hope. There are stricter measures, but all the basic functions of bankruptcy law are still in place.

Always remember, there are ways to deal with your business debts if you find yourself struggling under their weight. If there weren't, *I wouldn't have a business.* Also remember that there's no substitute for building your business carefully and correctly with a solid business plan, keeping in mind the legal ramifications of your debt structure as I've discussed in this chapter.

When I began my business, it was just me with my wife as the office manager. We avoided any debt whatsoever. We would literally count the number of appointments we had coming in, look at the cash flow, and determine what we had to spend on the business out of that.

We stayed that way a long time and it helped us to build a very healthy legal business. In our St. Louis home office, we now have six attorneys and twenty-five people in our office support staff. We've handled about thirty thousand bankruptcies in fifteen years and expanded our operation to offices in Kansas City, Detroit, Memphis, and Miami; we expect to open offices in several other cities this year. I feel proud of what we've accomplished, but when you think about it, we kind of had to succeed. It's really embarrassing when a bankruptcy lawyer has to declare bankruptcy!

So keep your entrepreneurial spirit alive and keep moving forward. Just build a strong base to move forward *from*. Feel free to contact me and find out about our services at www.DebtSecretBook.com. We're in the business of keeping everyone in business.

ABOUT JAMES BROWN:

Missouri consumer bankruptcy attorney James R. Brown has devoted his career to representing individuals against a credit industry that consistently finds way to squeeze more money out of the average hard working American. In addition, he has taken that same drive and determination to battle the insurance companies that take advantage of families who have been involved in serious car and truck accidents.

He has been married for 25 years and has three wonderful children. His hobbies include golf, travel, and reading. He has been involved in youth hockey for the past ten years as a coach and as a member of two youth hockey boards serving the St. Louis community.

He is licensed to practice law in Missouri and Illinois, and is a member of NACBA (National Association of Consumer Bankruptcy Attorneys), ABI (American Bankruptcy Institute) and NACTT (National Association of Chapter 13 Trustees.) Mr. Brown has been listed as a featured speaker at continuing legal education programs and local area high schools. He has been selected by the U.S. Bankruptcy Court to be a member of committees to draft official rules of the Court and a model Chapter 13 Plan.

Mr. Brown has opened offices in St. Louis, MO, Kansas City, MO, Detroit, MI and Miami, FL. Mr. Brown is the author of three consumer guides that focus on bankruptcy and personal injury law:

- *Get Out of Debt: What Your Creditors Don't Want You to Know*

- *10 Must Know Secrets To The Life You Dreamed of After Bankruptcy*

- *A Must Have Guide to Accident Cases in Missouri: 5 Costly Mistakes That Can Destroy Your Injury Claim*

In addition, Mr. Brown has co-authored a book with Virginia accident attorney Benjamin Glass: "**The Truth about Lawyer Advertising**."

For more information about the law firm, visit us at

www.DebtSecretBook.com

WHEN MIND SHIFT HAPPENS: "YOU'RE GOING TO DIE TONIGHT"

by Dr. Scott Schumann, DDS

You never know what's going to change your life. For me, it was the extremely strong possibility I was about to lose mine.

With a small practice that did okay. I wasn't making a lot of money – because, believe it or not, I gave away a lot of freebees. Yeah, I would often treat friends and family and not charge them – to the point where it was sometimes hard for *me* to pay *my* bills. The fact is that I love dentistry so much that I would do it all day for free – and I managed to prove that, over and over again, much to my accountant's dismay.

In 2003, I was trying to move things to the next level. I was setting up a new practice in Grove City just 8 minutes south of Columbus, Ohio – and I had just gotten married. It had been two months since the wedding and the new practice was just about to get going, when, in December of that year, a routine gall bladder operation turned into the nightmare of my life.

The operation was completely botched. Parasites got into my system, damage was done to my liver and my pancreas, and suddenly, things didn't look real good for me. Now I'm 6'3" – a pretty big guy who usually hits 225 on the scales. This medical ordeal had me down to 150 lbs, which made me resemble a walking skeleton, which is not a particularly good look unless it's Halloween.

Fortunately, my new bride was amazing through this. During the next three months I spent in the hospital, she slept in my room every night but one. Unfortunately, I couldn't seem to turn the corner to recovery. And one fateful night, two of my surgeon friends, who were helping to consult and repair things after the bad surgery, came to me and said that I needed to, as they used to say in the old movies, "get my affairs in order." In other words, call in my lawyer *that night* and sign some final papers.

Why? Because I was probably going to die before morning. They added helpfully that I *should've died the night before.*

When you hear that from two good friends, friends that you goof around with on a regular basis, your first instinct is – hey, fun is fun, but this kind of joking around isn't exactly the best medicine. But the punch line here was that they were dead serious. And, within hours, I might soon be just plain dead.

My new wife began to cry her eyes out. I was too stunned to speak.

Well, I did make it through that night, but the prognosis still hadn't changed. I asked my pastor to come in the next day, which he did. Normally, I'm not big on church rituals and practices, but, when he came to visit, I requested he lead a prayer session with me, which he did. That was the turning point.

Opening New Doors, Closing Old Ones

That night – another one in which I fortunately did *not* die – I grappled with a lot of the negative emotions that had previously held me back in my life. And I got past them. Moreover, I got motivated. If I survived this, I was suddenly determined to take charge of my life and *do well*. I had a new wife who stood by me even though she hadn't had a chance to have much of a marriage yet – and I had two new employees – one of whom I hadn't even met yet, since she was hired while I had been in the hospital – who were counting on there being a business to employ them. I wanted to make good for all of them – and I wanted to make good for *me*.

As you can probably guess by now, I did survive. (Otherwise, this chapter would have to be dictated through a medium). But it took a lot of time to get back to full health. For instance, I had to learn to walk and drive all over again. Overall, though, ever since that fateful night when I took stock of myself… *everything got easier*. I felt committed – and deep down, I was positive that if I was allowed to live through all that, it was for a reason and I needed to fulfill my potential. And for the first time in my life, I felt like I could.

I call this my *Mindshift*. I was suddenly open to learning. And changing. I attended business coaching courses and mastermind groups. While driving I listened to motivational/business CDs. I sought out people above me for advice and counseling, not people on my same level or below, and I would ask them, frankly, what and how can I do things to be better?

In short, I asked for honest criticism and I got it. I made myself vulnerable to go through that process and get something out of it. I finally walked into the new practice I had begun to set up before the hospital horror show six months later, in June of 2004. In the next six

179

months, I did more business than I did in all of 2003.

Why? Because I changed my approach and attitude to my practice. Before, I was lazy about marketing and running a business properly. I enjoyed doing what I did as a dentist and thought, in a hazy "Field of Dreams" way, that if I built it, they would come. In other words, if I was just a great dentist, my practice would grow on its own.

But it turned out that if you didn't *tell* people about your practice, they wouldn't come - because they didn't know you were there. If you didn't work with your staff to provide the best overall patient experience, you might not build the strongest customer loyalty. And if you didn't do the nuts-and-bolts work to create a profitable business, well...you probably wouldn't.

One of the most important changes I made was no longer to put so much energy into providing free dentistry. One CD I listened to said that if I became a better businessman, worked on my practice overall, and not just in it but on it, I would eventually have time to do as much free work on my friends and family as I wanted – even more. That prediction came true.

The name of this book is "Shift Happens." Well, the economy may have just shifted in the last year or so, but my mindset shifted back in 2003. And that prepared me and my practice for this downturn. Since 2003, my practice has grown 8 times its original size. Our revenues have grown by an average of 40% every year. And I still have more than enough time to help friends and family when I can – as a matter of fact, last year, I did over $100,000 worth of free work without it hurting my bottom line.

A big part of all that success is that I took the time and made the investment in reeducating myself about business and motivation. It used to be that I was afraid to take that time – I was worried that I couldn't afford to be away from work that much and, frankly, I thought it would bankrupt me. I've come to realize that taking those breaks to reenergize myself and my practice makes me more productive when I get back, helps me to improve my business and helps me to become more successful.

Building And Training My Dream Team

Another important element of my success was building and motivating my office staff. I think it's really important that the team you employ actually enjoys hanging out together – that they mesh as people. Now, a lot of that is just plain chemistry. I spent a lot of years banging my head against the wall trying to change people who just didn't fit in with what I was trying to do or with the rest of my staff. When it doesn't work, it doesn't work and I've learned to quickly recognize that.

On the other hand, what does already work you can make even better. Every quarter I make sure we do a group activity that has nothing to do with the office or the practice. It could be going to an Andy Warhol art exhibit, a George Clinton concert, a Red's baseball game or an OSU football game– as long as it's fun and everyone can enjoy socializing with each other. It bonds the group and helps get them through hectic workdays, knowing they can count on each other.

At the same time, you have to tackle your day-to-day business with your team and have them be accountable – to themselves and each other. If something didn't get taken care of, we look at that and decide how we make sure it does get covered next time. We review our internal business numbers every day and see how we can do better the next day.

Another thing I try to avoid is what I call the "Busy Bartender" syndrome.

You know how you go into a bar and the bartender is too busy to serve you? Or address you? Or even *look* at you and acknowledge your existence? That's not cool – it's bad customer service. I tell my team that you always take the time to at least acknowledge to a patient that they have to wait a minute or two to get what they need – otherwise it's upsetting.

Then there's the "Bad Boyfriend" syndrome. A guy goes out with a woman, has a great night, and then doesn't call her the next day. She thinks, maybe he's invoking the three day rule and waits it out. After three days, he doesn't call. As a matter of fact, he doesn't call again *at all*. At that point, in the woman's mind, he just becomes a jerk. And I could think of about five hundred stronger words than "jerk," but you can use your own imagination. Well, when we don't do follow-up calls to patients, we turn into jerks – or the word of your choosing – as well. It looks like we don't care and that we're just using them to make money. Again, it's *bad* 'good customer service' and it needs to be addressed.

I loved playing basketball, so that's what I use when thinking about building an office team that plays at a championship level. On a basketball team, if someone on your team is not in the correct position while playing defense and is about to get beat, a little push to help him get to the correct place can make all the difference. He may not like it, but it's nothing personal – it's about performance, what's best for the team. But sometimes, initially, it's hard for your employees to see it that way. You can, however, get an assist from the most unlikely sources.

For example, one of my team members was a bit irritated about being guided or corrected, and was trying to rely on her past experience as a way to evaluate herself daily. Our Office Manager was frustrated with the situation, and at a loss to resolve it, until she came across an article in *Cosmo* while getting her nails done, one that reviewed evaluating businesses with metrics/numbers. The Office Manager called me all excited that she came across something that echoed our Vital Factors training and had found a way for the person to accept the guidance based off her numbers. This made it especially non-emotional; numbers are a great way to evaluate a worker's or team member's performance and production. It took a manicure and a woman's magazine to make the *Mindshift* that time – but I'm grateful for whatever does the trick!

And apparently, what I'm doing with our team did the trick too – because this year, my office staff won "Best Team" in a nationwide contest held by Ed O'Keefe's Dentist Profits organization earlier this year. They beat out 1200 other dental offices – and that's an incredible honor.

Their prize was a trip to Disney World – and I added on some extras to that. I upgraded them to a nicer hotel and also paid for a half day at the Disney Institute so they could take some training courses. But mostly, it was a great free vacation and they had a blast.

Building a strong team means I don't have to micromanage – and I'm free to concentrate on my dentistry and building my business. And that's how it should be. When it comes to tough times, having the best possible team with the best possible training is a definite edge in surviving and even thriving. If you can help them make the *Mindshift*, you'll have a team whose performance you can be proud of.

Coping With The Economic Shift

Yes, I've managed to build a strong practice with an award-winning team. But I still have to watch the bottom line during this downturn. Columbus hasn't been as hard hit as some areas, since it's mostly a white collar work force – but the new economy means there are more reasons for patients to say "No" to dental treatments. So we have to continue to 'up our game'.

Part of that is getting back to basics and making sure we're doing our core business right. That's why we apply the ongoing metrics and staff accountability at my practice – to keep our performance as sharp as possible.

Part of that is also continuing my education and my growth as a businessman and a motivator. I continually strive to take my practice and my team to the next level. Standing still doesn't work for me – because I know we can keep doing things better and continue to grow the great practice we've created.

I'd like to share former General Electric CEO and business guru extraordinaire Jack Welch's six areas he tells businesses they need to concentrate on during this economic shift. I agree with them wholeheartedly and I've focused on them myself:

1. **Keep costs in line**

2. **Prepare for the worst-case scenario**

3. **Cash is King**

4. **Leadership needs to communicate like never before**

5. **Love your best people**

6. **Buy or bury your competitors**

I'd like to comment on two of these points, starting with Number 2. One of the things I've been concerned about is the fact that one large company financed for us a significant chunk of our business. What if that company chose to stop lending money? We would lose that business that was financed and what would replace it? What would that do to our overall practice? Would I have to lay off people?

That "worst case scenario" motivated me to go out and find two additional companies that could finance our patients' dental work – which means, at the moment, we now have three on board and are looking to add a fourth to offer as many options as we can to help our patients receive the dentistry they need to achieve a healthy, functional, and gorgeous smile.

Then there's number 6. In my area in this year alone, there are seven new dentists who have opened up shop. That means seven more choices for potential patients. So I have to continue to market aggressively – because I sure can't afford to buy out seven other practices!

So it comes down to the "bury" option. And to be honest, I used to worry about what the competing dentists thought of how I marketed my practice. Was I being too aggressive or treading on their turf somehow? But I finally decided that if they weren't paying me and I wasn't married to them, and as long as I was fair and honest in what I said and did, then I didn't need to fixate on their opinions of me.

Example - when I opened up my current practice, nobody in the area was that familiar with my name. So I named it for the area it was located in – and called it Grove City Dental. Another local dentist who used a similar name got extremely upset with me. He thought I should have named my dental practice after the street on which I am located vs. using the city's name. It got so bad that he was badmouthing me to everyone he knew – which, of course, ended up getting back to me.

I was worried about him damaging my reputation – until I saw how my practice was booming in terms of patients and growth. I realized that most people just wrote off his harping on my practice's name as meaningless complaining. The lesson to me was to focus on doing what you do as best as you can – and don't sweat the people trying to knock you down while you do it. Putting your energy into that negativity will only interrupt your own momentum.

And putting energy into your own negativity will also only result in you short-circuiting yourself. As weird as it sounds, I have to be thankful for the operation-gone-wrong back in 2003 and the resulting near-death experience. That was the *Mindshift* I needed to happen. And as a result, other external shifts are a lot easier to cope with.

I believe if you make the change inside yourself, then you can withstand the changes in the outside world. When *Shift Happens*, take stock of what you need to do to adapt. Take action. Make your own personal *Mindshift* – and good things will happen.

ABOUT DR. SCOTT SCHUMANN, DDS:

Dr. Scott Schumann, a native of Columbus, Ohio, grew up loving the Buckeyes, playing sports, and collecting rocks. Dr Schumann and his wife Robin live in downtown Columbus with their dog Bourbon the boxer. Dr Schumann loves supporting the local arts, sponsoring little league teams, golfing, fishing, attending concerts and NASCAR events.

Dr. Schumann graduated from the Ohio State University Dental School in 1989 and then completed his residency training at the University of Texas Health Science Center at San Antonio in 1991, a phenomenal experience, being trained and certified in advance dental techniques, dental implants, and sedation dentistry. He also received a fellowship in Hospital Dentistry, helping him to excel in assisting his medically compromised patients. After returning to Columbus Ohio, Dr. Schumann started his career and began teaching in the Advanced Dentistry Clinic at the Ohio State University, teaching dental residents advance cosmetic, implant, hospital, and sedation dentistry for ten years.

An active member in the Columbus Dental Society, Ohio Dental Association, American Dental Association, Academy of General Dentists, American Academy of Cosmetic Dentists and the American Dental Society of Anesthesiology has been very beneficial in keeping him and his team up to date on the latest developments in dentistry.

Dr. Scott Schumann's office in Grove City, a suburb 8 minutes south of downtown Columbus, Ohio, is often referred to by clients as "fun" and "cool." Dr. Schumann and his staff are well known for their love of helping their patients achieve the smile they always dreamed of. His highly trained professional team and office, with amazing new technological advancements, makes each patient visit as fun as possible without guilt or embarrassment.

Dr. Scott Schumann, of Grove City Dental, is one of only a handful of participants selected for America's PremierExperts® class of 2009. The participants selected to participate in this year's program are forward-thinking business owners, authors, speakers, entrepreneurs and corporate CEOs looking to separate their brand, increase revenues, lock out their competition and capture a distinct advantage over competitors in their market.

Dr. Scott Schumann has been published in multiple research journals, chapters in Oral-Facial Emergencies, featured in The 21 Principles of Smile Design, and Shift Happens. He has presented at various super conferences and study clubs. He has been quoted in The Wall Street Journal, USA Today, and Newsweek and will be appearing in Fall of 2009 on America's PremierExperts® TV show on NBC, CBS, ABC and FOX. Additionally, Dr. Schumann was recently interviewed on the radio show The Next Big Thing®.

IN TOUGH TIMES, FOCUS ON YOUR BEST ASSET

 *by* Dawn McIntyre

A s the founder and CEO of BoldlyBeautiful.com, an organization dedicated to helping women access and celebrate their true beauty, you might wonder exactly what I'm doing here in a book about surviving a massive economic down shift. After all, what can a beauty expert possibly tell you about dealing with tough financial times? We are better known for our recipes on how to make skin treatments from things you can find in your refrigerator.

My answer is simple – a lot more than you think. And I promise to leave your fridge out of it completely.

In the work I do with women all over the world, I do dispense my share of traditional beauty tips. It's part of my business and something that the clients who visit my site expect, and come to me for advice and help, appreciate. Still, the bulk of my work isn't about makeup, or skincare, or keeping up with the latest fashion trends. Bottom line, *it's all about self-esteem.*

Many of the women I work with first come to me because they're feeling unhappy, or unattractive, or that something about the way they look or feel just isn't right. And what's usually at the root of the problem is low self-esteem.

It's not like this is a huge surprise. We women are bombarded every day with images of 16-year-old, size zero models with airbrushed perfect skin and hair. For the 99.9% of us who are not 16, size zero, or airbrushed, it can be hard not to feel that we are somehow inadequate, or that we fail to meet some impossible standard of beauty. That's where the low self-esteem comes from. Of course, you probably already knew that.

But what you might not know is that this low self-esteem actually does affect the way women look. When we feel ugly, we hide ourselves in shapeless clothing. We don't do our hair. We lose the sparkle in our eyes. We don't smile. Worst of all, we don't feel joy inside, so we don't radiate that joy back to the world around us. It's like a light has been turned off inside us.

I see my job as empowering my clients to turn their light back on. I help women move beyond the artificial images they see on TV and in magazines to access and celebrate their own true, real beauty. I teach them techniques to help them shut off the negative messages and focus on the positive so that they see the good and the beauty that's in each of them – because it is in all of us.

Ultimately, my job is about helping women everywhere to become the best they can possibly be - both inside and out. It is about giving their minds and souls, as well as their bodies, the support they need to truly shine that light, and look and feel their most beautiful.

So, what does all this have to do with the economy? Stick with me. I'm getting to it.

Through my work with women of all shapes and sizes, colors, races, and ages, one thing has emerged as an absolute constant. No matter who a woman is, the better she feels about herself and the world around her, the higher her self-esteem is and the more beautiful she looks. Of course, self-esteem isn't just about beauty.

For example, say you're a man. Your appearance is probably fairly low on the list of things that you consider essential to your self-esteem. And I don't want to discriminate or generalize, because plenty of women feel that way too. For many of us, our sense of self-worth is all tied up in what we do. It's all about questions like: Am I respected? Am I making money? Am I successful?

When our work life is going well, when we're on top of our game, when we have the money to buy the things we want as well as the things we need, we feel powerful. We feel in control. And we feel good about ourselves.

But when the opposite happens – when we lose a job, or watch a business struggle, or see our savings or investments dwindle away, we can feel powerless. We feel like all we can do is watch what we have built slip away. And for many of us, that feeling of powerlessness goes hand in hand with low self-esteem. And the light inside goes out.

It's not like anyone can be blamed for letting this happen. It can be hard to have faith in ourselves and our abilities when everything around us seems to be going wrong.

But when our "professional" self-esteem collapses, when our confidence light goes out, just like with beauty, the negative messages we send ourselves become their own self-fulfilling prophecy. Tell yourself you are ugly, and you may very well look ugly. Tell yourself that you're a failure, or a victim, or that you're powerless over your circumstances, and chances are you will be all of those things as well. That's the power of self-esteem.

But luckily, just like negative thoughts and messages have their power, positive ones do too. The key is to learn to do with business what I do with beauty. Harness the power of the positive – find a way to make the most of your situation – and it can help you turn this economic shift into a blessing, regardless of how it has affected you so far.

For example, it's easy to spend time dwelling on what's gone wrong. But what if you spent that time telling yourself that you deserve to succeed, and that you will use this time to focus on your success? Suddenly, you have a purpose; you have something to do. You've given yourself an opportunity. And you've put yourself back in control.

So what can you do with this control? Ideally, you can turn this difficult time into a chance to grow and change, and become better and stronger than you ever were before. You can come out of this crisis poised to reach even greater levels of success than you had before things went wrong. You can gain your confidence back, and turn the light inside you back on.

That may sound hard to believe, especially if you're having a hard time just paying the mortgage or putting food on the table. And trust me, I don't live on another planet. I know we all need to deal with our most basic needs first. The thing is, I truly believe that every challenge that we face in life is actually an opportunity. <u>Meaning that somewhere in the midst of all this financial craziness, an opportunity is waiting for you. And I believe in my core that it's an opportunity to put some time and energy into your most important asset; one that often gets neglected in the rush that often comes with success. *It's finally your turn to do some work on you.*</u>

Chances are, when your business is booming, you don't have a lot of time to focus on self-improvement, or even, in some cases, self care. So when things come up that you really want to do or should do for yourself – in a business or a personal sense – you have to put them off until some mysterious time in the future we all know as "later." You'll take that yoga class or get yourself back in shape or learn how to relax "later." You'll take stock of your life and how to get more of what you want "later." You'll learn a new skill that will make you better at what you do "later."

If your business has slowed, if you have time on your hands, if you've lost a job, you've just been handed a huge opportunity. Because that "later" just became now.

Now, when your phone isn't ringing off the hook and you can find time in your schedule to devote to something other than work, you can find some time that's all about you. Time to take stock of where you are in your career and your life and think about where you want to be when things get better.

Have you been on the right path? Now is the ideal time to prepare yourself to get back in the game when things turn around, which they will, sooner than you think. So take time now to think about what you do well, about what you're good at, about what your strengths are - to focus on them and remind yourself of them. And think about what you need to work on to come back even stronger.

Take the courses you need to improve your skills. Take the time to get your body in shape. Eat healthier foods. Start exercising. Remind yourself every day of the gifts you have, and remind yourself to honor those gifts by not wasting a single day, or even a single moment, dwelling on how bad things are. Instead, take all of that energy and the time you've been given and use it to get ready for the next phase of your life.

If, after taking time to assess your life, you decide you aren't happy with where you were and the way things were going, this time truly is a gift. Because now, you can take time to change course and to think about where you truly belong and where you will really be happy. You can focus on what you really want out of life and what it takes to get there. And most of all, you can remind yourself to celebrate the strengths and talents you have, and honor them by doing all you can to develop them and give them their due.

Remember, even if you don't feel particularly successful right now, you have the power inside you to do and be what you want. So look at this economic shift as a gift to take time to learn to be the very best you can be. Because before you know it, things will have shifted again.

…And then you'll be too busy!

ABOUT DAWN MCINTYRE:

Dawn McIntyre, Professional Spiritual Intuitive, is an expert in leading men and women into higher states of expansion and beauty consciousness.

Dawn is regularly sought out by the media. She has been featured on ABC, CBS, NBC and FOX as well as being featured in USA Today, Newsweek, The Wall Street Journal and numerous other publications. She was also a regular guest on BTV in Edmonton, Alberta for two years.

Dawn is also the best-selling author of Big Ideas for Your Business (Celebrity Press 2009) and is the forthcoming author of two books (1) Bouncing Back - Thriving Through Changing Times - due to be released in the fall of 2009, and (2) The New10 - Beauty Redefined ....a 40 Day Program to Your Infinite Beauty and Perfection of Being, due to be released in February 2010.

Dawn lives in Calgary, Alberta with her daughter, Kennedy.

Dawn has launched her exclusive member's community at:

www.BoldlyBeautiful.com